MORE

SPOOKY
Campfire Tales

Also in the Spooky Series by
S. E. Schlosser and Paul G. Hoffman

Spooky California
Spooky Campfire Tales
Spooky Canada
Spooky Colorado
Spooky Florida
Spooky Georgia
Spooky Indiana
Spooky Maryland
Spooky Massachusetts
Spooky Michigan
Spooky Montana
Spooky New England
Spooky New Jersey
Spooky New York
Spooky North Carolina
Spooky Oregon
Spooky Pennsylvania
Spooky South
Spooky South Carolina
Spooky Southwest
Spooky Texas
Spooky Virginia
Spooky Washington
Spooky Wisconsin
Spooky Yellowstone

MORE

SPOOKY

Campfire Tales

*Tales of Hauntings, Strange Happenings,
and Other Local Lore*

RETOLD BY S. E. SCHLOSSER

ILLUSTRATED BY PAUL G. HOFFMAN

gpp

Guilford, Connecticut

398.2
More

Text copyright © 2014 by S. E. Schlosser
Illustrations copyright © 2014 by Paul G. Hoffman

Editor: Meredith Dias
Project editor: Lauren Szalkiewicz
Layout: Justin Marciano
Text design: Lisa Reneson, Two Sisters Design

Library of Congress Cataloging-in-Publication Data is available on file.

ISBN 978-0-7627-9034-0

Printed in the United States of America

10 9 8 7 6 5 4 3 2 1

For Judy, who spent her early childhood
with the ghost of Pearl White.

For my family: David, Dena, Tim, Arlene, Hannah, Emma,
Nathan, Ben, Deb, Gabe, Clare, Jack, Chris, Karen, Davey, and
Aunt Mil. And for my honorary sister, Barbara Strobel.

For Erin Turner, Paul Hoffman,
and all the wonderful folks at Globe Pequot Press,
with my thanks.

Contents

Contents

Introduction

I sat near the campfire, watching with amusement as the kids tried to roast the perfect marshmallow. Too close to the flames and the marshmallow caught on fire; too far away and it wouldn't melt. I chuckled when my niece's marshmallow blazed up, charring instantly while she frantically tried to blow it out. Across the fire, my nephew was roasting his marshmallow to perfection. When it was done, he placed the nicely browned treat on a graham cracker, layered a chocolate bar and another graham cracker on top, and presented the s'more to me. I complimented him on his roasting technique and accepted the snack with gratitude. He gave me a quirky grin and went over to the table to grab another marshmallow from the bag.

Behind me, a band was warming up. Party guests roamed the carefully mowed fields behind my brother's farmhouse, looking at the animals, playing games, talking, laughing, eating. As the band swung into its first number, I contentedly crunched my s'more. The second annual September Embers was off to a good start.

As darkness fell, more people gathered near the campfire, until a big crowd sat around roasting marshmallows and talking.

Inevitably, someone called for a campfire story and everyone automatically looked at me— the author of multiple spooky folklore books. Dang! I should have left the campfire before it got dark.

Caught with a marshmallow in my mouth, I was unable to voice a protest when my sister-in-law nominated me as first up in the evening's entertainment. Fortunately for us both, I had quite an arsenal of spooky tales. The problem was deciding which story to tell. Should I discuss the "Mothman," who hunts unsuspecting victims on the back roads of West Virginia? What about the Pennsylvania antique hunter who inadvertently bought "Bloody Mary's Mirror"? Or the "The Ghost of Pearl White," who nightly ascended the steps of her former boardinghouse?

"Tell us about Estrid," my niece called.

"I don't know," I said dubiously. "That story is pretty scary. Do you want to hear a scary story?"

Everyone roared, "Yes."

The response was unanimous and shouted so loudly that it rocked me back in my chair.

"Estrid it is," I said when the tumult died down.

So they wanted a scary story, did they? I'd make it so scary none of them would sleep tonight. I rose with an evil grin and began my tale.

For the hearty souls who made it through "Estrid" without fleeing, I told the story of "The Girl in White," who appeared at a dance and tried to take one of the men back to the grave with her. This was followed by "Collateral," in which an impoverished couple takes a loan from a stranger named Vladimir who literally sucks them dry. To end the storytelling portion of the evening, I asked the group to help me solve the mystery of the "Seventh Window" and what lay behind it.

Exhausted and rather hoarse, I grabbed lemonade from the cooler and ceded the floor to a comedian who shortly had everyone laughing. Satisfied that I would not be missed, I slipped away.

The tales in this spooky book, collected over multiple research trips, come from many different cultures scattered throughout the United States. The stories range from mildly spooky to keep-the-lights-on scary, so folks can choose the "scare" level that is appropriate for their audience. Some of my favorite spooky legends are here. I hope you enjoy retelling them as much as I do.

—Sandy Schlosser

PART ONE
Ghost Stories

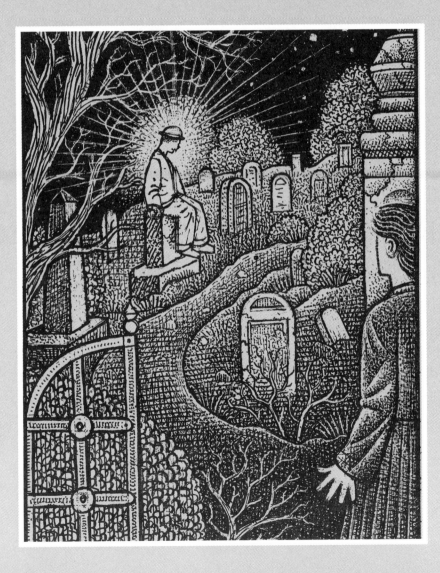

1

The Ghost of Pearl White

When I was a kid, my grandparents bought an old boardinghouse in Jersey City, New Jersey. It had once housed actresses working for a big silent film studio located directly across the street, but the film studio was long gone, and now the boardinghouse was unused. My grandparents converted it into a three-family home. They moved into the bottom floor, offered my parents the second floor, and rented out the third. It worked out pretty well for everyone. There was extra income for my grandparents; privacy for our family, with quick access to Grandma when it was wanted or needed; and a quiet couple on the third floor who provided additional income for my grandparents with no hassles.

Actually, the couple upstairs was a little too quiet. It was odd. No one's life could be that serene.

I was not sure how the idea got started in my small head— maybe I overheard my parents talking—but I soon got the notion that the wife in the upstairs apartment was a recluse. Occasionally, my parents or grandparents would encounter the husband on his way to or from work, and he always chatted with the family for about ten minutes on the day he delivered the rent check. But the wife never appeared at all.

My parents sometimes speculated about this strange woman they never saw, but I didn't pay attention to their conversations.

I was more concerned with dolls and school friends and playing in the sandbox in our backyard than with reclusive adults, so I ignored the whole situation.

Now, bedtime for me at the new house was 8:00 p.m. sharp. My bedroom was opposite the main staircase, and I could see it clearly when lying tucked up in my bed for the night. One evening about a month after we moved in, a strange lady wearing a gorgeous, fancy yellow dress strolled past my room at 8:15 p.m. and walked up the third-floor staircase.

I sat up in bed, mouth open in surprise. Who was *she*, and where had she come from? I shivered, for the air was suddenly cold in my bedroom. I was a little frightened by this strange person strolling calmly through my new house as if she owned it. I was about to yell for my mother when I realized who the woman must be. She was obviously the reclusive wife of our third-floor neighbor. I relaxed at once and lay back against the pillow.

She sure was a pretty lady, I thought as I drifted toward sleep. *And that dress was to die for!*

A couple of nights later, the lady strolled past my door again at 8:15 on the dot. This time she wore a pink dress with elaborate lace and carried a fan. I sat up and watched her with interest, rubbing my arms against the sudden chill in my room as she walked up the staircase and disappeared from view. I wanted my mother to make me a dress like that. I wondered if the reclusive third-floor lady could tell my mother the store where she had bought it. I snuggled under my covers with a smile. Maybe the store sold dresses like that in my size.

After that I saw the lady almost every night. She strolled past my door and walked up the third-floor staircase until she

THE GHOST OF PEARL WHITE

disappeared from sight. I loved the lady's clothes. Often she wore the yellow dress in which I'd first seen her. But sometimes her dress was blue or pink or white, with lovely lace or embroidery. *She must work in a very fancy store,* I thought. My mother never wore such long, fancy dresses, and she never wore her hair up with combs and jewels.

One night, about a year after we moved into the old boardinghouse, I was awakened from a deep sleep by a cold breeze that flapped the curtains on the window and rattled the coloring books on my desk. I blinked sleepily and saw a figure walk through my bedroom door. It was the lady from the third floor again. She was wearing the fancy pink dress with the fan, and her hair was pulled back with two lovely pearl-white combs. The woman walked over to my closet and went through the partially opened door. I blinked in surprise, for it seemed almost as if her body had gone through the wood of the door itself, rather than through the small opening between the door and the frame. But that was silly. No one could walk through wood! And why had she gone into my closet?

The cold wind ceased as abruptly as it began, and my sleep-fogged brain refused to wrestle with the mystery. I'd seen the lady every day for more than a year, and she'd never bothered me before. If she wanted to spend the night in my closet, so be it. As sleep claimed me, I decided that there must be a secret staircase in my closet that led to the third floor.

When I woke in the morning, I jumped out of bed and went into my closet. Sure enough, the lady wasn't there. I started tapping the walls and the ceiling, trying to discover the key to the secret door, but it eluded me. I'd have to ask the lady the next time she went upstairs at 8:15. Of course, I completely forgot about the secret door in the closet by bedtime, too caught up in my childhood dramas to remember the strange event of the previous night.

A few weeks later, my grandparents sold the old boardinghouse to my aunt and we moved into a nice home in the suburbs. So I never solved the mystery of the secret door in the closet.

About a month after the move, my aunt came stomping into our suburban house in a rage as I sat at the kitchen table, eating my after-school snack.

"I cannot believe you sold me a haunted house," my aunt said to my grandpa.

"What do you mean haunted?" Grandpa asked.

My aunt explained. Loudly. And in great detail. She ranted about the ghostly woman who walked up the third-floor staircase every night at 8:15 p.m. on the dot. And the previous night, the ghost had walked right into my aunt's room—my former bedroom—and had floated past her bed and right through the closet door.

I stared at my aunt, pop-eyed in amazement. The lady with the beautiful dresses had been a *ghost?* I could hardly believe it. I shivered a little, remembering the strange breeze that had fluttered the curtains of my room the night the lady walked into my closet. Then again, maybe I *could* believe it.

"You're crazy, Loretta. You must have been dreaming," my father said.

My grandfather shook his head sadly as he contemplated his poor, addled daughter and added, "Daughter, there is no such thing as a ghost."

Realizing I had to defend my beleaguered aunt, I told my parents and grandparents about my own ghostly sightings. In the end they had to believe it, because both my aunt and I had seen the ghost many times.

A look through old photographs of female stars from the silent film era identified the ghost as that of Pearl White. Further research revealed that my closet had been the dressing room for some of the actresses. So that explained why the ghost had sometimes walked into my closet. (To own the truth, I was a bit disappointed that there was no secret staircase.)

To this day, I still have no idea why the ghost of Pearl White walks the halls of her old boardinghouse. Perhaps it is to remind herself of a happy period in her life? All I know for sure is that Pearl White is the best-dressed ghost in Jersey City! I'm still envious of her beautiful gowns.

2

Ghost in the Stacks

I saw the girl out of the corner of my eye while I was studying in a remote section of the second-level stacks in the library. She was pretty, with reddish hair and pensive, wide eyes on an intelligent face. She wore a red-flowered dress with a white button-down sweater. I straightened up, patted my hair to make sure it was smooth, and took another look. The girl was gone. Vanished into thin air. My shoulders sagged a bit as I turned back to my books. Oh well. There were more important things to do, like studying hard so that I got into medical school when I graduated next year. Pretty girls could wait.

Still, I kept seeing the girl's face whenever I closed my eyes, and I kept looking around as I exited the library, hoping to see her again. She dominated my thoughts as I staggered down the front steps with my heavy backpack.

Then a few of my friends shouted to me, interrupting my romantic thoughts, and I walked over to their gathering place.

"Where've you been, Tony?" my friend Jeff called.

"At the library," I said, patting my backpack for emphasis.

"You have been *studying?*" Jeff asked incredulously.

I grinned. "I've gotta crack down now so I can get into med school," I replied to his jibe. "Can't always be partying with you losers!"

That set them off, as I had intended, and kept the jokes flying until dinnertime.

Although I didn't admit it to myself, I chose the same spot in the stacks for my studies the following afternoon, hoping to see the pretty girl again. This time, I was in luck. After about an hour, she appeared among the shelves, browsing intently. I noticed that she was wearing the same dress and sweater that she'd worn the previous day. *She must like that outfit,* I thought.

Obviously, it was time for me to do some browsing too, I thought, straightening my shirt and rising casually. I turned left and then right before walking into the line of bookshelves where the pretty girl had just been browsing. Then I stopped abruptly. Where had she gone?

I was astounded. *The girl must move with amazing speed,* I thought. It had taken me only a few moments to rise and move through the aisles, but in those short seconds she had managed to move silently away without me seeing her. She was probably into sports if she could move that fast. Maybe she played soccer, just like me.

I walked casually through the stacks, glancing this way and that, trying to spot her again. No luck. With a sigh, I turned back to my seat and my studies, a frustrated man.

I didn't see the girl again for several weeks. Finals were rapidly approaching, so I spent hours in the library—many of them searching for and daydreaming about the girl in the red-flowered dress. But she never appeared.

Finally, I abandoned hope of ever meeting her and buckled down for my last week of review before finals. The girl wasn't even on my mind the day I rushed out of the stacks toward my friend Jeff, who was impatiently beckoning for me to hurry

GHOST IN THE STACKS

up. Then I saw the pretty girl rising from a seat in a far corner. I stopped abruptly in shock, for she hadn't been sitting there when I had gone to my study desk on the other side of the room.

I turned, hoping to catch her eye as she moved into the stacks, but she did not look my way. *This is it, boy,* I told myself. *If you want to meet her, you'd better do it now.*

Ignoring Jeff, who was calling my name impatiently, I followed the girl into the stacks, eyes fixed on her dress and the attractive swing of her reddish-blonde hair. She turned the corner and I quickened my step. I turned the corner too and stopped, baffled and a little spooked. The girl had vanished again.

I shivered. This was getting creepy. Was the girl avoiding me? Why? We had never spoken, and I certainly could not be accused of staring at her, as I had only seen her for a total of maybe thirty seconds! Shaking my head at the mystery, I went over to Jeff—who was loudly demanding an explanation—and exited the library.

Later that week I decided to skip the big football game to cram for finals. Just about everyone else was at the game, so the library was nearly deserted as I strolled over to my favorite study spot in the stacks on the second level. I'd decided I was going to ignore the pretty girl with the reddish-blonde hair from now on. Obviously, some things were just not meant to be. Besides, it creeped me out, the way she kept vanishing into thin air.

I was engrossed in my studies when I heard books and shelves tumbling to the floor. I leapt up and ran toward the sounds. To my horror, the pretty girl whom I'd been trying to meet lay on the floor with books all around her. She was unconscious, and my heart gave a painful thump when I realized that there was blood staining her red dress. Then, right before my eyes, she

11

vanished. I sat down abruptly on the floor, my legs shaking too hard to hold me up, realizing that the girl in the red-flowered dress was a ghost.

It was then that I remembered the story of the girl who had been murdered in the library back in the sixties. I knew at once that she was the ghost I'd seen. I had just seen a paranormal reenactment of her final moments of life. I buried my face in my shaking hands, feeling a terrible grief at the tragic loss of such a beautiful girl. From what I had heard, her murderer was never apprehended. It made me furious to think that justice had never been served.

Slowly, I uncoiled my body and rose to my feet. The aisle between the stacks was empty now, the books mysteriously returned to their shelves. I was too unnerved to remain in this deserted place, so I grabbed my books and went back to my room.

I saw the ghost one more time before I graduated. I was reading at my favorite study desk when I felt a chill in the air. I shivered and looked up. And there was the ghost of the pretty girl, standing a few feet away from me. Our eyes met, and I saw fear and despair in her face. My own face twisted in sympathy. Impulsively, I stretched my open hand toward her. At the sight of my distress, she reached her hand back toward me and gave me a tiny smile. For a moment, I felt the touch of cold fingers on my warm ones. Then she was gone.

3

Sachs Covered Bridge

I don't know what exactly draws me back to Sachs Covered Bridge each time I visit Gettysburg. I just know that I feel compelled to drive there and take pictures. Of course, it is a beautiful spot—a covered bridge that was used by the Confederate army to cross the creek when they withdrew from Gettysburg. But how many pictures can you take of the same place? Well, okay, if you're a photographer, that's a silly question! Hundreds, in all weather, seasons, lighting . . .

But, really, I'm only an amateur photographer, so why I personally felt compelled to take so many pictures of the bridge was a mystery about which my boyfriend was obsessing as he drove through the darkening countryside one evening in the late fall.

"You've visited this bridge about a hundred times already," he complained, rounding a bend at full speed.

"But you've never seen it," I countered.

"Come on, honey. I'm hungry," he said. "We can see it tomorrow. Or the next time we visit Gettysburg."

"No bridge, no dinner," I told him crisply.

Visiting Sachs Covered Bridge was part of my Gettysburg tradition, and that was that. Besides, the bridge was supposed to be haunted, and that was definitely part of its draw for me. You never knew what might happen on a haunted bridge!

According to legend, three Confederate soldiers convicted of being spies were hanged from beams in the covered bridge, and their bodies were discovered by Union soldiers patrolling the area. Their spirits were still said to haunt the bridge, especially at night. Other folks claimed they sometimes smelled General Lee smoking his pipe when they were standing on Sachs Covered Bridge. I'd actually smelled pipe smoke there once myself, and that was one of the reasons I kept coming back to the haunted bridge.

As we approached the bridge, a chill blasted over my skin in spite of the warmth flowing into the car from the heater. The bridge, usually a friendly spot, seemed sinister and dark this evening. My stomach turned over, and I swallowed back nausea. It felt as if there was a foul presence on the bridge that did not want us to intrude there.

"I changed my mind," I said quickly as my boyfriend stopped the car. "I don't want to take pictures here after all."

"What?" my boyfriend practically screeched, staring at me in amazement. "After you made such a big fuss about it? After you forced me to look at every single solitary picture you ever took of this bridge before we came to Gettysburg? No way, honey! I could be back at the hotel eating dinner and drinking beer right now, but no! We had to come to the bridge! Out you go to take your photos!"

He was right, I guess. It was silly to come all this way and not take the pictures. But I was utterly terrified to step out onto the bridge! My hand shook as I reached for the door handle, and it shook again as I secured my camera. Praying with all my might that whatever dark power was out there would leave me alone, I leapt out the door and aimed my camera practically at random down the length of the bridge, which was completely empty of everything but me and the car as I took several snapshots. But I could feel someone—a very nasty someone—standing right behind me, willing me to leave or die. The presence throbbed at me in an almost physical way, and my skin crawled desperately. I didn't dare turn around. I couldn't. I just whirled my camera around, aimed it over my shoulder, and snapped a picture—fast! Then I leapt back into the car before whoever—or whatever—decided to grab me. I gasped, "Get me out of here now!"

My boyfriend took one look at my white face and terror-filled eyes and got me out of there. I didn't stop shaking until we were safe in our hotel room for the night.

When I loaded the digital pictures onto my laptop computer the next morning, I went immediately to the pictures of the Sachs Covered Bridge, unsure of what I would see. In the first photo, a little boy in period costume stood an arm's length away from the camera. He was glaring at me with a twisted little face and an evil grin. He certainly hadn't been there when I took the picture, yet he looked solid enough to be real. The second photo was filled with misty figures that looked like phantoms. Creepy! I shuddered as I looked at them and quickly went to the next photo—the one I had taken over my shoulder without turning around. I gave a shriek of fear that brought my boyfriend crashing into the room.

"What is it?" he shouted, and I pointed a shaking finger at the screen of the laptop. Pictured on it was a filmy dark figure—half human, half beast—with blazing orange eyes filled with such menace and hatred that it made my stomach roil. He

SACHS COVERED BRIDGE

appeared so close to the camera that he must have been directly behind me. He looked like the Devil.

My boyfriend's eyes widened, and he gasped, "Delete it. Delete it now!"

But how could I delete it? I had captured pictures of ghosts on my camera. Was it worth the fright I'd had? I wasn't sure about that. Still, I couldn't delete them.

My boyfriend refused to look at the photos again, and he swore never to take me back to Sachs Covered Bridge. But I may go back there someday myself.

4

The Whirlwind

In hindsight, I suppose it wasn't a good idea to go ancestor-hunting in the local cemetery at dusk, but that's when my friends and I got the notion, so off we went as soon as we thought of it. My mother had told me we had kin in the cemetery, but I'd never gone there before.

We got on our bikes and skimmed expertly through the tourists who thronged the streets of Key West in the winter. It was getting dark when we turned up the street where the church and cemetery stood. It was shadowy and mysterious. I shivered in delight and sped up the road, leaving my friends behind. They shouted and pedaled hard until the three of us rode abreast. We skidded to a halt by the church and parked our bikes by the cemetery gate.

"This is a pretty spooky place," my friend Amanda said uneasily, brushing blonde hair nervously from her forehead.

This was true, but I decided to ignore the fact. Amanda was a bit of a scaredy-cat. If we acknowledged her fear in any way, she'd turn and run. So Terry and I ignored her comment as we slipped through the gate and made our way through the rows of headstones.

Around us, the shadows grew longer and darker as we started reading surnames, trying to locate my kin. The Spanish moss dripping from oak tree branches overhead thrashed like writhing snakes in the sea breeze, reminding me a bit of the tale of Medusa. I shivered a bit and then scolded myself for being a scaredy-cat like Amanda.

"Here's one," Terry called, beckoning me to a rather dilapidated old tomb. I wandered over to take a look. By now the sky had grown so dim that I had to plaster my face up against the stone to read it. Hmm. The dates looked correct. "This may be one of my great-grandparents," I said, straightening. I could barely see Amanda, who was in another aisle of tombstones.

A chill breeze sprang up, whipping the hair from my neck and making goose bumps rise on my arms. It really was spooky here. "We need a flashlight," I said to Terry, who was trying to read the grave next to my great-grandparents' tomb.

"Susannnn . . ." Amanda called my name suddenly. I looked over at her and gasped, my body freezing in disbelief. A whirlwind full of dead leaves and dust was blowing up from the ground in front of Amanda. She staggered backward, desperately trying to get away from it, her hair and clothes whipping about from the ferocity of the breeze it created. A sepulchral voice rose out of the whirlwind, roaring wordlessly in rage. The sound rose in pitch, higher and higher until my brown curls stood on end.

Beside me, Terry shouted in panic and ran toward the cemetery gates. "Come on," she called over her shoulder to Amanda and me. I forced my legs into action, sprinting after Terry. But when I glanced back, I saw that Amanda had tripped over a low tombstone and lay directly in the path of the shrieking whirlwind.

I raced back and grabbed her arm, trying to get her moving again. Amanda gasped and scrambled upright, but fear made

THE WHIRLWIND

her clumsy and she fell again over a jagged stone, cutting her knee open. The blood that spurted from the cut was suddenly illuminated by a bluish light that appeared directly above the whirlwind. It coalesced rapidly into a glowing man in the garb of an old-time Spanish settler. The spirit gave a shout of rage at the sight of me and Amanda and swooped toward us, arms outstretched.

Amanda gave a shriek and found her feet at last, racing away from the ghost so fast she left me far behind. I sprinted after her, my way uncannily lit by the glowing phantom behind me. The air around me was so ice-cold that it made my lungs ache as I ran. I leapt over a large tombstone that stood between me and the gate. Amanda and Terry were already on their bikes.

"Hurry, Susan! Hurry," Terry shouted. I raced through the gates and stumbled into my bike, knocking it over. As I grabbed it off the ground, I risked a backward glance and saw the phantom hovering just inside the gate, the whirlwind somehow mixed up with his glowing form. Dust whipped into my face as I jumped onto my bike and followed my fleeing friends. By the time we reached the end of the street, the phantom had vanished and the whirlwind had died away. We kept going.

Terry's house was closest, so we rode there and collapsed on her porch, panting.

"There is no way I am ever going back to that cemetery," Amanda gasped. "What was that thing?"

I shook my head, but Terry said, "I heard that the ghost of the man who single-handedly drove all the pirates out of Key West haunts the cemetery, but I thought it was just a myth—you know, one of the stories you tell tourists to freak them out."

"Worked for me," I jibed. "I am completely freaked!"

Beside me, Amanda groaned in agreement and poked gently at her bloody leg. Terry blinked, realizing for the first time that Amanda was wounded. We hustled her inside the house to clean up her knee. Then I rode home with her because she refused to go anywhere alone. I couldn't blame her.

It was completely dark when I headed back to my house. I stayed on the main roads, trying to keep out of the shadows. In my mind I kept seeing the glowing figure swooping at me and feeling the supernatural coldness piercing my lungs. I decided then and there that I'd had enough ancestor-hunting. From now on, I would stay away from that graveyard!

5

Haunted Tower

My Great-Uncle Powhatan was once a colonel in the Confederate army, until he was injured in battle in 1864. "Uncle Pow was shot in the head," Mama told my twin brother, Frank, and me when we were little. "His mother nursed him right here on the plantation. She brought him through alive when everyone thought he was dead, but when he woke from his coma, he had no memory of his life before. He didn't even know his own mother. The head injury left him a bit simple, so you must be very kind to old Uncle Pow."

Uncle Pow told the best stories in the world, and he was stronger than a team of oxen. He towered over us—six feet six inches in his bare feet—and loved to swing us around. He never remembered much of what happened on any given day, but that never bothered us. The adults treated Uncle Pow as if he were touched in the head. But to Frank and me, Uncle Pow was a war hero, and we were immensely proud of him.

Each summer, Uncle Pow took us fishing on the river, and when we were twelve, he helped us build a fort in the woods near the ruins of the haunted shot tower. Technically, we weren't supposed to go near the shot tower, which was dangerously decrepit and half sunken into the ground, its door long buried

HAUNTED TOWER

beneath soil and creepers. But Frank and I loved visiting the tower because it was said to be haunted by the spirit of a woman who wept and clawed at the walls, begging for someone to let her out. It gave us shivers every time we looked at the tower. We talked about visiting it at night to see if we could see the ghost.

Before we could try it, Mama found out about our fort and scolded us fiercely for disobeying her and dragging poor, simple Uncle Pow into our illicit schemes. "It's dishonorable to take advantage of an old man who can't remember things because of a head injury," she said. "I'm ashamed of you boys!" As punishment, she gave us extra chores for an entire month.

Frank was flattened by Mama's words. We'd been dishonorable. We'd taken advantage of Uncle Pow's head injury. It was a hard condemnation to bear.

"I'm going to become a brain doctor and fix Uncle Pow's head so he remembers everything he forgot," Frank told me at the end of our twelfth summer. Lighthearted Frank was so serious that I believed him at once.

True to his word, Frank studied hard and got into a famous university. He studied some more and got into medical school. Then he went to Europe to study with a famous brain surgeon and learned everything that science could teach him about the brain.

Almost fifty years to the day after Uncle Pow was brought home to the plantation with the wound that shattered his skull and his wits, Frank came home from his sojourn in Europe and told the family that he could heal Uncle Powhatan.

"It is a very simple surgery," Frank told the gathered family. "Six times out of ten, the person's memory is completely restored."

We were dubious. Uncle Pow was happy as he was. Wouldn't it be kinder to let things be after all this time? All the people he'd known and loved fifty years ago were long gone now. But Frank was adamant. He'd spent his life studying medicine so he could help Uncle Pow. No one would stand between him and his goal. And no one did. Uncle Pow was brought to the hospital, where he beamed proudly at his great-nephew-the-doctor and told the nurses lovely stories about the animals he cared for on the plantation. No one could have been happier going into surgery than Great-Uncle Powhatan.

Frank and I were both beside him when the old man woke after the surgery. He blinked hazily and stared from face to familiar face, a pucker between his eyebrows.

"Where am I?" he snapped briskly after inspecting us for a long moment. "What is this place?"

It was the voice of a stranger. Gone was the happy smile, the languid tone. His voice was deeper, with the authoritative tone of a colonel.

"Where are my men?" Uncle Pow demanded. "Did we win the battle?"

He gasped suddenly and struggled to sit up. "Annabelle! I must rescue Annabelle. She's all alone in the tower!"

Alarmed, we pushed Uncle Pow back onto the bed. Frank said: "It's us, Uncle Powhatan. Frank and Tom. Remember? We are your great-nephews."

"Don't talk nonsense. I have no nephews. My sister is an infant," the old man cried. He thrashed about so fiercely that he knocked both of us to the floor. As the nurse came running with a sedative, Frank and I stared at each other in horror. Uncle

Pow didn't remember us. His past had returned in full, but he retained no knowledge of anything that had occurred after his accident!

The old man calmed under the sedative, but not for long. When it wore off, he began thrashing again, crying, "Annabelle! My wife! Annabelle. You must help her!"

Frank and I stared at each other again, this time in consternation. Great-Uncle Powhatan was married? I'd known him all my life, and no one had mentioned a wife.

For three days the old man thrashed and screamed whenever he came out of sedation. No one could calm him, and he recognized none of his family. Uncle Pow grew weaker each time he regained consciousness, and it was soon apparent that the old man was dying in great agony of mind and spirit.

Frank's agony was as great as that of the old man he had spent his whole life trying to help. Hoping his home environment might ease his suffering, Frank brought Uncle Pow to the plantation, where Mama and I shared the burden of caring for the old man in his last days.

Frank and I were with Uncle Pow when he woke on the fourth afternoon after the surgery. As consciousness approached, Uncle Pow's face contorted with pain and his right hand crept to his head to claw futilely at the bandage. A spasm of remorse crossed Frank's face as he clutched Uncle Pow's hand and begged him to rest. Uncle Pow's eyes shot open when he heard Frank's voice. Taking in his white coat and air of authority, Uncle Powhatan pulled Frank close to him.

"Listen to me, doctor," he gasped. "I am dying, and there isn't much time. I am a colonel in the Confederate army. I was given a few hours' leave between battles to go to church and marry my sweetheart, Annabelle, who lived in the town where our division was camped. We met at the church. Annabelle was wearing a blue silk wedding gown, and I was all slicked up in my best Confederate uniform. After the wedding we went down to the river with a picnic lunch for a few hours of honeymooning before I was due back at my camp. Suddenly, we heard a terrible blast from the woods in front of us. Annabelle thought it was an approaching thunderstorm, but I knew the sound of cannon fire. The Yankees were attacking my base camp."

The old man fell back on the pillows, gasping for breath. Uncle Pow coughed repeatedly, and blood leaked from the corner of his mouth when he spoke again. "I had to get back to my men, but I couldn't abandon my new wife. The battle was almost upon us when I thought of the old shot tower. Acrid smoke stung our nostrils and bullets winged through the air as we ran across the meadow."

The old man fell silent a moment, eyes fixed on some spot over Frank's shoulder, his face a rictus of remembered terror. "There was a dry cistern in the tower. I lowered Annabelle into it using an old rope. 'I will be back in a few hours, my dearest love, as soon as the soldiers are gone,' I told my Annabelle. Then I covered the cistern with the stone lid, leaving my wife alone in pitch blackness, and ran back into the woods, hoping to rejoin my company and defeat the Yankees before they found my bride's hiding place. I must have been shot as soon as I left the tower, because the next thing I remember is waking up in this hospital."

The old man's eyes focused suddenly on Frank's face. "It's been days since I left Annabelle in that black cistern," he cried. "There was no food or water down there. Please, you must go to her. You must rescue her! Run, boy. Go *now!*"

Uncle Pow's body arched in a sudden seizure and a moment later he fell dead against the bedclothes. Frank stared at the old man's corpse in horror. Then he ran. He had to. The force of the old man's last words thrust him out the door and down the stairs before conscious thought kicked in. I followed, as compelled by the old man's story as Frank appeared to be. We did not slow when we reached the toolshed, even knowing that whatever had happened to Annabelle had happened long ago. Frank threw hammers and saws and lumber out of his way, frantically searching for a shovel.

"I'm sure someone heard her cries and let her out," I said to Frank as he grimly thrust a pickax at me. Frank grabbed a shovel for himself and raced away without answering, galloping down the river path that led to our childhood fort.

I followed at a run, remembering all the stories I'd heard about the haunted tower. Folks said the ghost became very active during a thunderstorm, screaming and scratching and begging for help. And Uncle Pow had said that Annabelle mistook the canon fire for an approaching thunderstorm. . . .

Oh, dear God! Was *Uncle Pow's wife* the origin of the ghost story?

Frank reached the dilapidated tower ahead of me. He started shoveling around the half-buried door as I attacked the hardened turf with my pickax. When the sunken door was revealed, Frank kicked his way through the rotted wood and grimly tore away miles of rustling dead vines that hid the stone cover in the floor. It took all our combined strength to lift the cover, and I marveled that a young Uncle Pow had moved it alone.

As we opened the pit, we were overwhelmed by the smell of musty old air and perfumed decay. A ray of golden light from the setting sun pierced through the shattered remains of the tower door and shone into the cistern at our feet. I stared in horror at the huddled heap of bones and blue silk, which was all that remained of my great-aunt Annabelle. There were deep vertical gouges in the wall above her skull where she's tried to claw her way out of the black pit. And a golden wedding band gleamed on the bones of one hand.

6

The Ghost's Cap

A full moon hung in the star-speckled sky as Anya climbed out her second-story bedroom window into the cold autumn night and shimmied down the bare oak tree. The chilly air didn't bother her. She was on her way to the graveyard to win a bet against the supercilious Ivan and his annoying little sister. The prosperous children of a local farmer, Ivan and his sister often took pleasure in teasing Anya about her worn clothing and old boots. But this time the joke was on them. Ivan had bet the fancy silver buttons from his best coat and a yard of handmade lace from his sister's petticoat if Anya could learn the name of the ghost that sat on a tombstone in the local cemetery from midnight until dawn each night. Because Anya didn't believe in ghosts, she was going to invent some nonsense to tell the gullible Ivan and his sister. But first she must walk to the graveyard past Ivan's house; she knew they wouldn't believe her story unless they witnessed her nighttime journey firsthand.

A wild wind shook the treetops as Anya stalked past Ivan's house. She made certain her face was clearly visible under the streetlamp, knowing that Ivan and his sister were watching from the window to see if she was brave enough to take them up on their bet.

At the gate to the cemetery, Anya paused uncertainly, seeing a white figure seated on a gravestone partway down one narrow aisle. The wind moaned around her, and she clutched her shawl close, shivering in the cold air. Then she realized the white figure must be Ivan, trying to trick her into believing there really was a ghost in the cemetery. Really, that boy! It was time someone taught him a lesson.

Anya pulled open the gate and stalked down the narrow passage between the gravestones until she stood in front of the white figure. Ivan had obviously taken some trouble with his disguise. The old man seated on the gravestone had his hands folded in his lap, and his white clothes glowed in the moonlight. His wrinkled skin was corpse gray, there were dark rings under his cavernous dark eyes, and he wore a white cap just like the one Ivan had described. That cap annoyed Anya. Whoever heard of a ghost wearing a cap? She reached out and pulled the moldering covering off the white figure's head, crying, "You don't frighten me. You are not a corpse! You are a saucy boy who just lost all his silver buttons to me!" With that, she danced away between the tombs, waving the moldy white cap triumphantly above her head.

When Anya got home, she tucked the cap under her arm, nose wrinkling from the musty smell of decay, and climbed back up the tree to her window. She threw the moldering white cap through the window into the darkest corner of her room and slid in after it. Closing the window against the cold air, Anya slipped into her nightdress and went to bed. She didn't hear the wind pick up shortly after she fell asleep, nor did she see a white figure floating outside the window, peering in at the glowing white cap in the corner of the room. "Give me back my cap," the figure called, tapping the glass with a shimmering finger. "Give me back my cap."

Anya turned over in bed and covered her head with the pillow, ignoring the tapping sound at the window. "It's just the branches of the oak tree," she told herself sleepily.

"Give me back my cap," the figure called again. It rattled the window with a decaying hand as Anya snuggled deeper into the covers. "Give me back my cap!" The wind gusted against the house, shaking it from top to bottom. But Anya slept on.

"My cap!" howled the floating ghost. Its cry was taken up by the autumn wind and blown all over the village, making dogs howl and cats yowl and the good farm folk shiver in their beds. But Anya did not stir. She knew there was no such thing as ghosts.

Dawn came and the glowing figure vanished with a frustrated pop. In the dusty corner of Anya's bedroom, the ghostly light faded from the white cap.

After breakfast, Anya went to Ivan's house to collect her bet. "I went to the graveyard," she said, "and I met the ghost of Old Peter. He gave me this hat as proof!" She waved the cap in the faces of Ivan and his sister. Ivan stared glumly at the decrepit white cap, which was filled with grave dust and mold. Sadly, he cut the silver buttons from his fine coat, and his sister removed the expensive lace from her petticoat. They gave their prized items to Anya, who danced triumphantly away with the buttons and lace in her pocket and the foul white cap on top of her yellow curls.

THE GHOST'S CAP

On her way home, Anya grabbed the smelly cap from her head and threw it into the river. "Good riddance to bad rubbish," she called as it sank beneath an eddy. "Honestly. Whoever heard of a ghost wearing a cap?"

That night Anya stayed up late sewing silver buttons on her coat and trimming her petticoat with lace. Then she bade her parents a cheerful good night and went to bed. Just before dawn, the wind howled and slammed into the old house, rattling every window and shaking every door. "Give me back my cap!" a white figure roared, hovering beside the oak tree. "Give me back my cap!" But Anya slept on, dreaming of her new silver buttons and lace.

In the next bedroom, her parents woke in fear, hearing the ghostly voice howling like thunder just outside their house. "Give me back my cap," the floating figure shouted in rage. The wind slammed the shutters again and again. The air in the bedroom grew so cold it burned the nostrils and made the parents' breath crystallize into a fog around their heads. The figure hovering outside glowed with an eerie blue-white light that illuminated every corner of their room.

"What is that thing?" screamed the mother, hiding beneath the covers. Trembling from head to foot, the father stumbled to the window and shouted, "In the name of God, tell us what you want!"

"I want the cap your daughter stole," cried the ghost, his eyes blazing silver fire. Tiny lightning bolts raced up and down his white garments. Anya's parents cowered away from the terrible figure floating in wrath outside their window. Then the first ray of dawn crowned the hill behind the house, and the spirit vanished.

Anya's father raced to the room next door and dragged his daughter out of bed. "Where is the cap you stole from the ghost?" he shouted.

Anya stared at him sleepily. "What do you mean, Father?" she asked. "What ghost?"

"The ghost outside our window," cried Anya's mother from the doorway.

"That's not a ghost, that's Ivan," Anya said with a yawn. "He's playing tricks again."

"Even that trickster Ivan cannot float ten feet above the ground," her father said. "Now tell me where you put that cap!"

"I threw it in the river," Anya said. "Honestly, what a fuss!"

"Threw it in the river. Ah me! The ghost will destroy us when it finds out," cried the mother, wringing her hands. "Father, you must go for the priest."

The mother scolded Anya soundly while the father fetched the local priest and explained the situation to him. The priest stared gravely at the erring Anya, who glared back, annoyed by this unnecessary fuss.

"You must come to the church now, and we will ring the bell for Mass so the good citizens can pray for your soul," the priest said. "If enough of us pray, the ghost may leave you alone."

"What nonsense," grumbled Anya as her parents dragged her to the church. The priest rang the bell, and the local residents came to pray. The priest made Anya kneel in front of the altar while he read a prayer for the dead. Behind her, the good people of the town listened gravely, staring at the defiant girl who dared deface the dead.

All at once a massive whirlwind blew in from the south. Black clouds darkened over the sky, the trees bent double in the blast, and then the church was shaken by a blow like that of a giant's hand. The doors blew open and the whirlwind howled inside, tossing hymnals and Bibles and candles and icons to the floor. The walls shook, the stained-glass windows shattered, and the congregation fell to the floor. At the altar, Anya gave a bloodcurdling scream as the lights went out.

All at once the roaring wind and the earthquake stopped. A loosened portrait thudded to the floor in the silence, and a candle toppled from its holder and rolled to the foot of the altar. The eyes of every person in the room followed the candle as it stopped at the empty railing where, moments before, Anya had knelt in a defiant rage. There was nothing there now save a few long golden curls, a handful of silver buttons, and a bit of lace.

7

Underground

We'd timed our visit to Oregon to coincide with the Pendleton Round-Up and had managed to snag one of the very last hotel rooms in town. My husband, a big rodeo fan, was as excited as a little kid to be attending the famous Pendleton Round-Up. Myself, I was eagerly anticipating a tour of the famous—or should I say infamous?—Pendleton Underground.

According to the literature I'd read prior to the visit, Pendleton was a small village first settled in the 1860s or thereabouts by a fellow named Goodwin. It was mostly a farming community that didn't begin to boom until prospectors found gold in the Blue Mountains. After this discovery, Pendleton became a stop for supply wagons, as well as an entertainment capital where miners could spend their hard-won gold and where cowboys and ranchers could come to drink, gamble in the thirty-two saloons, and visit one of the eighteen bordellos.

Chinese workers came in abundance to work in the mines or do business in town. They were not always welcomed by the general populace, so they burrowed underground and began digging tunnels from business to business, cellar to cellar, living and working in the tunnels they had dug. It was estimated that Pendleton's labyrinth of underground tunnels, dug by the Chinese between 1870 and 1930, wound for more than seventy miles beneath the town. Through the years, the Pendleton underground tunnels and rooms were used by Chinese workers, Prohibitionists, opium addicts, ice-cream stores, butcher shops, speakeasies, saloons, card parlors, and even a bowling alley!

Rumors abounded about the Underground. One story claimed that a pair of train robbers who used the tunnels to store their ill-gotten goods had died in the dark passages under an old house during a gun battle over the stolen gold. It was said that the ghosts of the robbers still haunted the place, and people could sometimes hear them crying, "It's my gold!"

I shivered in delight as I recounted the legend to my husband. Being pragmatic, he just laughed. But he did agree to accompany me on the tour of the Pendleton Underground.

I picked up the phone at once and booked the very next tour. My husband laughed as I bounced on my toes in excitement and danced around the hotel room, as giddy as a child. I was acting even sillier than he had on the first night of the roundup!

After a quick lunch, we went to the tour headquarters and gathered with a large group of people, all interested in the story of the mysterious tunnels beneath our feet. I told my husband that we were probably standing over a tunnel right now. The tour guide heard me and confirmed that part of the Pendleton Underground was directly below us. I grinned in triumph.

We watched a brief film, and then we were escorted outside. We walked around a corner and stopped so the tour guide could tell us a short story about the cowboys who had stood on that very spot and called up to the working girls in the rooms above our heads. I craned my neck upward, trying to picture the scene. Above me, something scarlet flickered in and out of view at the corner of my eye. I blinked and rocked back on my heels, chills running down my spine. For a moment, I'd stared into bold black eyes over a gaudily painted red mouth. The flash of scarlet had been dyed feathers framing an attractive heart-shaped face.

I stared openmouthed at the empty window above me until I was jostled by the moving crowd around me. Everyone else was walking down the steps beside me.

The skin between my shoulder blades pricked with apprehension as I blindly followed my husband down the staircase. What had just happened? Had I imagined the face in the window?

We went through a door and found ourselves in a cellar that once housed a saloon. I shivered as the temperature around me dropped more than ten degrees. It was cold in here. I wished vainly for my sweater, left back in the hotel room, as I stared at the re-created Old West scene. Cowboy mannequins lounged around tables and played cards, while our tour guide stood behind the polished bar and discussed the role of the saloon in the days of the gold rush. My husband was absolutely fascinated.

I listened with half an ear as I poked around the basement room and looked at the exhibits, trying to imagine what it was like to drink and play cards underground, a lump of gold in my pocket and a gun at my side. The tour guide beckoned us onward, and I trotted obediently behind my husband, who was chatting eagerly with a rodeo enthusiast.

When we entered a re-created Chinese laundry, I was hit with a wave of not-quite-nausea. I swayed as my eyes swam with strange, out-of-focus colors. My stomach flip-flopped strangely, my spine went rigid, and the skin on my shoulders and arms prickled with goose bumps. For a moment, I could hear water swishing, and, beside me, a man's voice said something in Chinese. I gasped and whirled, but no one was there.

As suddenly as it had come, the nausea faded and my head was clear again. The room swam back into focus, and I realized that the rest of the tour had moved next door into the re-created ice-cream shop. I followed hurriedly. My husband motioned for me to keep up.

Spooked by my experience, I stayed by his side as the tour guide discussed the use of this space for ice-cream storage and then took us through a doorway into a long underground room full of small cots and benches. The room was lined with windows that looked out onto a tunnel-hallway lit by glassed-in openings in the sidewalk above.

The guide stepped into the room, which housed a demonstration of the famous Pendleton wool industry, and spoke knowledgeably about the exhibit. A loud buzzing like the noise of a large drill prevented me from hearing much of the talk. Some workmen must be fixing an exhibit, I supposed. I glanced around in annoyance and whispered to my husband, "I wish they'd stop drilling." He blinked in surprise and whispered back, "What drilling?" That's when I realized the buzzing sound was only in my head.

I shrugged, and my husband turned his attention back to the lecturing tour guide. Around me, the buzzing sound grew louder and became a flood of words and phrases in broken English and Chinese. My stomach turned over as strange bits of color flashed first here and then there in the room. For a brief moment, I saw an almost-invisible Chinese man doing calculations on an abacus made of some kind of black wood.

The hands—the only clearly visible part of the man—were rapidly moving red beads back and forth on little wooden bars.

"Come on, Sally. Don't lag behind," my husband said impatiently, pulling at my hand. Instantly, my vision cleared and I was back in the present. I staggered and clutched the wall for a moment. Then I followed my husband through the door and into the tunnel itself, which was constructed of dark basalt stones, smoothed fairly flat on the outside and carefully mortared together. I could see through the large windows right back into the room where we had just been standing. I glanced toward the place where I had seen the hands holding the abacus, shuddered once, and resolutely kept my eyes forward as we navigated around a corner and into the next area.

We passed through a place where a thriving butcher's shop had conducted its business. I blinked cautiously as I looked around the room, but everything stayed in focus, for which I was grateful. It was fascinating to see the old posters advertising low prices for meat, the old-style cash register, and the cold room where the meat was kept. I was feeling much more myself now, having thrust aside the odd occurrences to think about when we were aboveground.

Then I stepped into the next room, an old card room that had been used as a bar during Prohibition, and heard an alarm bell jangling desperately from somewhere overhead. In front of me was the re-created scene of a card party, with rough-looking fellows sitting around a table, eyeing one another suspiciously. Above the mannequins, the little bell was still vibrating, as if the string that activated it had just been pulled. No one else seemed to notice the vibrating bell or the sound of feet thudding rapidly. I tensed, wanting to run away with the fleeing feet.

My husband noticed my distress and whispered, "Are you all right?" I nodded slightly, unable to speak, and gratefully followed the rest of the tour down another tunnel and into a brighter room once used as a bowling alley. Then we were back on the street in the fresh air, and I was panting with combined fear and exhaustion. What was happening to me? Was I losing my mind?

My husband was very concerned. "You look ill, honey," he said. "Do you want to go back to the hotel? We can take the rest of the tour another day."

"I'm fine," I snapped a little sharply. How could I explain to my pragmatic husband that I was seeing things in the tunnels? He'd put it down to tiredness or say I was coming down with something.

The tour headed down the street toward the old bordello, which was the next stop. I followed determinedly, so my husband went with me. Taking hold of my hand, he eyed me sideways once in a while to make sure I was all right.

We climbed the "steps to heaven" and toured the rooms of the old bordello without any distressing color flashes or visions on my part, though I thought my husband's eyes would fall out when he saw some of the decorations on the walls. Then we were at street level again, watching our guide open the locked door leading to our last stop on the Underground tour. I started to shake at the thought of going back underground. We were going to see a Chinese jail just below our feet. Apparently the Chinese policed their own in the early days. I drew in a deep breath and followed my husband downstairs into a musty room filled with bunk beds and tables and a cooking stove. There were Buddhas and Chinese hats on the top shelf by the stove.

UNDERGROUND

A gong hung next to me, and as I looked at it, the not-quite-nausea swept over me and the tour guide's voice faded away. I stared at the gong in a cowardly manner, listening to several male voices conversing leisurely in Mandarin Chinese behind me. I heard someone laugh—a merry sound—and finally turned to gaze at a jolly man cooking something over a stove that looked similar to the one in the re-creation. Behind him, a group of men sat around a table playing mah-jongg, and another man lit incense before a little altar in the corner. It was all so clear that for a moment I thought I could walk right up to the table and join the game.

From somewhere far away, I heard my husband's voice urging me along. I walked forward slowly, nodding to the men at the mah-jongg table. They beamed and nodded back, not at all surprised to see me. I risked a quick glance down and saw that I was wearing a dress and held a basket on my arm. I wondered who I was, back in this time.

I walked with my basket into a small side room once used as an opium den and set my basket down beside a man lounging languidly on the bed, smoking deeply from his pipe. He dreamily nodded his thanks to me, and my lips moved, speaking to him in Chinese, a language I did not know.

Suddenly, the brightness died from the scene. The bed was empty; the room was faded and musty. I stared in shock at the old platform where opium users had once smoked their pipes, willing myself back in time for just one moment more. Then my husband's hands closed on my shoulders, and he turned me to face him. His eyes were wide with worry, and I could feel his hands trembling against my shoulders. "Sally, what's wrong? You looked like you were in a trance."

"I . . . I think I should get out of here," I gasped, swaying slightly with vertigo. Coming back to the present day was a shock to my overwrought nervous system. My husband took my arm and half carried me out of the tunnels and up to the daylight world. I stood trembling for a long moment, gasping in the fresh air.

"Pretty creepy down there," my husband remarked, watching me closely. He didn't believe in the supernatural, but even he could tell something had happened to me. "You can tell me all about it when we get back to the hotel."

I nodded gratefully. I needed time to think about what I'd seen before I discussed it with anyone.

My husband guided me to the tour headquarters, where we thanked our guide and bought a souvenir book before heading into the sunlit street. As we walked back toward the car, I looked down at one of the purple-glass windows in the sidewalk that helped light the tunnels below. In my mind, I saw a pair of hands busy with an abacus and a man smoking a pipe full of opium. I'd never thought of myself as psychic, but I was convinced that I had truly walked into the past during my time in the tunnels below Pendleton. Glancing up at my pragmatic husband, I wasn't sure how much I should tell him. Would he believe me? I wasn't sure I believed it myself, and it had happened to me!

"What's next on the roundup schedule?" I asked, watching my husband's face light up as he grabbed the battered schedule from his pocket. Gesturing animatedly, he spread the paper on the hood of our car and started enumerating the possibilities. I leaned next to him and glanced through the information on the sheet, happy to put the ghosts of the past behind me and look to the future—which had better, I informed my eager spouse, involve some ice cream.

8

The Girl in White

He was sulking a little, standing at the sidelines while all the other men danced with their pretty partners. His girlfriend had not come to the dance that night. Her mother was ill, and so his girl had remained at her side. A fine pious act, he thought sourly, but it left him at loose ends.

His friend Ernesto came up to him between sets with a cold drink and some words of encouragement. "After all, Anita is not the only girl in the world," Ernesto said. "There are many pretty girls here tonight. Dance with one of them."

Bolstered by his friend's words, he started looking around the dance hall. His eye fell upon a beautiful young girl standing wistfully at the edge of the floor beside the door to the terrace. She was dressed in an old-fashioned white gown, and her skin was pale as the moon. Her dark eyes watched the dance hungrily from her position behind a tall fern, and he felt his heart beat faster. Such a lovely woman should be dancing!

He made his way through the bustling crowd and bowed to the girl in white. She looked startled by his addresses, as if she had not expected anyone to notice her that night. But she readily assented to dance with him, and he proudly led her out onto the floor for the next set, all thoughts of Anita gone from his mind.

THE GIRL IN WHITE

Ernesto and some of the other fellows laughed when he danced across the floor with the girl in white in his arms, which made him angry. Then a couple bumped right into them as they whirled in synchronization with the dance. He was furious and wanted to stop the music and make them apologize. But the girl in white only laughed and hushed him. "They couldn't see me," she told him. "No one can."

"I see you," he said warmly. "No one will overlook you again!"

She smiled and told him that he didn't understand. He put her remarks down to shyness.

When the dance was over, he hurried to get his fair partner a drink. Ernesto approached him at the refreshment table. "When I told you to dance, I meant with a partner," his friend teased him.

"I was dancing with a partner," he replied, irritated by his friend's remark. "The loveliest girl in the world!"

"You've had too much to drink, my friend," Ernesto replied. "You were dancing all by yourself out there!"

He glared at Ernesto and turned away without answering him. He made his way back to the girl in white and asked her to stroll with him along the terrace. The night was beautiful, the sky full of stars, and his heart was in his eyes as he stared at the girl in white gazing over the beautiful scene.

The girl in white turned to him with a sigh and said, "Thank you for the dance. It has been a very long time since I had such pleasure."

"Let us dance again, then," he said, infatuated.

She shook her head. "I must leave now," she said, catching up her skirts with one hand and drifting toward the stairs at the side of the terrace.

"Please don't go," he pleaded, following her.

"I must," she said, turning to look at him. Her eyes softened when she saw the look on his face. "Come with me?" she invited, holding out a pale hand.

His heart pounded rapidly at the thought. More than anything in the world, he wanted to go with this lovely girl. And then his subconscious mind, in panicked self-defense, pushed a clinical observation through his romantic befuddlement. In a moment of blinding revelation, he realized that he could see the stone wall of the terrace through the girl's outstretched hand.

His desire melted away with the shock of his sudden revelation: He had been dancing with a ghost! His eyes snapped back up to the girl's face. At his look of horror and disbelief, the girl gave a sad laugh and dropped her translucent hand.

"Good-bye," she said, her body becoming thin and misty. "Good-bye."

Then she was gone.

He gave a shout of terror, his heart pounding painfully against his ribs, as he realized how close he'd come to taking the ghost's hand and walking into death beside her. Sweat poured off him as he bolted from the premises, leaving his horse behind, and ran all the way home.

He told Ernesto the whole story the next day when his friend came to bring him his horse. Ernesto whistled in awe. "You saw the spirit of Consuela, my friend," he said. "She was an aristocrat's daughter who lived in this region more than a hundred years ago. She died of consumption the night before her first ball, and they say her spirit sometimes attends the local dances, hoping to claim one of the dances that she missed."

He shuddered at the thought of his dance with the ghost. "I will not be visiting that dance hall again," he told Ernesto. "And from now on, the only girl I will dance with is Anita!"

9

Lover's Leap

My grandfather sat silently at the far end of the table, listening as my parents raged back and forth across the good china, each blaming the other for my elder sister's elopement. I sat still as a stone as the cutting remarks grew louder, rattling the glasses. How could she have run off with a sailor? Where had they met? How long had this clandestine courtship been going on?

I glanced down the table at my tall, elegant grandfather with his lion's mane of white hair and broad, imposing shoulders. Our eyes met for an instant, and I immediately realized that grandfather knew all about my sister's elopement and that he would never share his knowledge with my parents. I dropped my gaze to my napkin to hide a grin. I'd known about my sister's romance from the start and had kept it hidden. Why should it matter whom Elaine married, as long as he was an honorable man who earned a good living and treated her well?

A mere decade ago, we Americans wrote a Declaration of Independence that said all men were created equal. If all men were created equal, than I figured it didn't matter if Elaine was a society lady and Charlie was a poor sailor. They should be allowed to marry. But my parents thought otherwise. Father was the younger son of a British aristocrat, and Mama had come from a wealthy Virginia family. Marrying outside one's class was just "not done" in their worldview. So Elaine had eloped with her sailor.

When dinner was finished, my grandfather rose from the table and called, "Take a walk with me, Thomas?" My father waved me away from the table with barely a glance, so I followed my grandfather into the hallway and the servant brought our coats.

As soon as I saw the full moon outside, my heart hammered with fear. I knew exactly where we were going, for it was the same spot my grandfather visited every month on the night of the full moon. We were walking to Lover's Leap to sit under the tall pine at the edge of the ravine and wait for the ghost.

The trees whispered in the night wind, and the shadows lengthened around us as we approached the narrow ravine. I hated this place. I had first heard the ghost scream at the tender age of six. The haunting began with a sudden, intense silence and a sharp drop in temperature until the surrounding air felt as cold as ice. Next, a loud cracking noise sounded from the top of an old pine tree that hung precariously over the ravine, as if a huge branch had broken in two. The cracking sound was followed by a terrible scream and the heart-stopping noise of a body plummeting into the ravine. The ghostly wail ended abruptly in a terrible thump as the screaming man hit the sharp rocks at the river's edge. It was followed by a loud splash as his dead body rolled into the river. Then there was silence.

It was a horrific death scene that played out every month under the light of the full moon. I never understood why my grandfather came here each month to listen to the tragic death replay itself again and again. He'd even installed a bench under the precarious pine.

LOVER'S LEAP

As we approached the aforementioned tree, a shock of sheer terror iced through my body. My heart leapt into my mouth when I saw a white figure stir in the shadows under the pine. My hands shook as a second shadow joined the first. Then my sister's voice called my name, and the relief was so intense that sweat poured down my neck and back as I raced to embrace her. Charlie stood next to us, beaming with delight as he shook my grandfather's hand.

"Congratulations on your marriage," the old gentleman said, waving them to a seat on the bench. Elaine and Charlie sat holding hands as moonlight streamed over the hills to the east. I sat on the pine needles beside the bench, leaning my head against Elaine's knee and watching moonlight flickering on the babbling water several hundred feet below our perch.

"Thank you for helping us," Charlie said to my grandfather. "I would not have had the courage to propose to Elaine if you hadn't given me your approval."

"I don't understand why you approve and Mama does not," Elaine added in her soft soprano. "I thought you, of all people, would want me to marry a rich man, to bring more money or consequence to our family."

Grandfather smiled and took a seat beside Charlie. "I have more money than I know what to do with. As for consequence, that is something your mother cares about. I value other things. Like family. And love." He paused and then reached into his deep coat pocket and removed a long box, which he turned over and over in his hands. Finally, he said, "Perhaps this wedding present and the story that goes with it will help you understand why I have given my consent to your runaway marriage."

Grandfather handed the box to Elaine. I watched curiously as she opened it and drew out a long, blue-and-white-checked bandana made of gingham. The homely old scarf was covered with the most intricate embroidery I'd ever seen. Delicate flowers and graceful birds filled every inch. The flowers seemed to shimmer in the moonlight as Elaine turned it this way and that, staring in fascination at the artwork stitched upon such an unlikely object. She handed the bandana to Charlie and removed a second item from the box, a slim silver dagger with a lovely design engraved upon the hilt. Charlie passed me the embroidered bandana and took the dagger from Elaine as my grandfather began his story.

"My younger brother was a sailor like you, Charlie," Grandfather began. "His name was also Charles, and he was a lieutenant in the navy."

I stared incredulously at Grandfather's stern face in the moonlight. "I didn't know you had a brother," I exclaimed.

Grandfather frowned at me for interrupting. "He died young," Grandfather said. "If I may get back to my story?" He cocked an eyebrow at me, and I subsided onto the pine needles as he told the following tale.

Lieutenant Charles Madison was a dashing figure—tall and blond and handsome with a roving eye and a honeyed tongue. The young ladies sighed with longing whenever Charles entered a room. He served as an aide to the admiral, and he sailed on the first Virginian flagship to enter the fabled realm of China.

One evening, the admiral and his officers were invited to dine with a powerful Mandarin and his high officials. They dined in a glittering palace filled with treasures and ate the most delicious and exotic food that young Charles had ever tasted. As the meal progressed, the handsome lieutenant became aware of rustling sounds and soft female whispers somewhere above his head. Glancing up, he saw a finely wrought ivory screen edging a high balcony. Small slits were cut through the ivory, and Charles thought he caught a glint of light in an eye pressed to a hole in the screen. Seeing his glance, a courtier told the lieutenant that the wives and concubines of the Mandarin were secreted behind the ivory screen, where they watched the strange white men who had come to their palace from a foreign land.

After protracted farewells, the naval officers exited the palace via the grand entryway. As Charles passed an elaborately painted screen, a hand reached out suddenly and plucked the blue-and-white-checkered bandana from his neck. Charles turned quickly and saw the edge of a silken robe disappear behind the screen. He shrugged off the theft and followed his fellow officers back to his ship.

The next day, a servant came aboard the battleship carrying a rice paper–wrapped package for Charles. When the lieutenant opened it, he found his checkered bandana covered on both sides with delicately embroidered flowers and birds. Charles put the bandana thoughtfully away in his inner pocket and went to the town to visit a certain fisherman who had befriended the Virginian when he first arrived in China. The old man examined the embroidered bandana closely and then told the lieutenant that it contained a message hidden in the embroidery, asking Charles to present himself at a certain side door of the Mandarin's palace at a certain hour that night.

Upon so presenting himself, Charles was introduced to Flower of Love, the enchanting young wife of the aged

Mandarin. Flower of Love had seen the handsome blond officer through the enclosed balcony screen and had fallen for the man so exotic in looks, so much closer to her in age. Every night at the conclusion of his naval watch, Charles would knock on the secret door of the palace and follow a servant through a perfumed garden to a small summerhouse, where Flower of Love awaited him.

What started as a daring adventure became a love affair that consumed the lieutenant's mind and heart. Charles went about his duties like a man in a dream. Nothing was real to him save Flower of Love and her night garden. His naval duties—once the center of his world—became a nuisance, a boring way to pass the time until evening fell. Charles was almost mad with his longing for Flower of Love. He begged her to run away with him, to leave her aged husband and come to America. When she agreed, Charles booked passage for two on a merchant ship, prepared to flee China with the Mandarin's lovely wife.

On the appointed evening, Charles packed his kit and stole away from the naval warship. After he entered the Mandarin's palace through the secret door, he made his way through the night garden to the summerhouse. As he stepped inside, Charles was seized from behind and bound hand and foot. His captors thrust a gag into the lieutenant's mouth, carried him to the inner courtyard of the palace, and threw him down at the feet of the Mandarin and his assembled household. Everyone was there—wives, children, servants, and soldiers.

Charles uttered not a word as he staggered to his feet, knowing that his fate was sealed. He squared his shoulders, determined to die like a man and an officer. A small smile fluttered briefly across the Mandarin's lips when Charles met his gaze squarely. He lifted his fan and snapped it open, the sound echoing around the silent courtyard like a gunshot. At this signal, a parade of servants marched through a narrow archway, leading Flower of Love between them. She was dressed like a bride in white and silver, with pearls and flowers in her black hair. Her exquisite perfume filled the air as she entered the courtyard with dignity and faced her Virginian lover with a smile of gentle pride. Something in her face and bearing warned the lieutenant that something terrible faced him—perhaps something even worse than death, though he could not fathom what that might be.

Charles cried out through his gag when the servants seized the Mandarin's unfaithful wife and tore off her bridal array before the silent eyes of his entire household. The soldiers seized Charles as he struggled to free himself and spring to the defense of the woman he loved. The servants grabbed the defenseless woman roughly by her bare arms and thrust her into the face of her American lover in the mockery of a kiss. Flower of Love was pressed so close to Charles that he could feel her warmth, smell her perfume, and see the love and resignation in her lovely dark eyes. Too soon, the servants pulled her away and stood her just out of arm's reach of her lover, facing her husband.

The Mandarin stepped down from his throne and bowed to the American naval officer. Then he removed the silver dagger from the lieutenant's belt and saluted him with it in the American style. Turning swiftly toward Flower of Love, the Mandarin raised the dagger. Charles screamed in horror against his gag. With one mighty thrust, the Mandarin cleaved his faithless wife in two from head to toe, disemboweling her before the eyes of her American lover as her blood spurted out over his uniform.

Charles stood transfixed with horror as the Mandarin cut out her heart and threw her body at her lover's feet. With a second bow, the Mandarin thrust the bloodstained silver knife back into Charles's belt and had the lieutenant dragged through the night garden and flung through the secret door where the love affair had first begun.

When Charles regained consciousness, he was aboard his naval vessel, which was already many leagues out to sea on its way home to Virginia. Charles left the service when he reached Virginia and never spoke of his time in the Orient except once, in private, to his older brother. But he kept the silver dagger and the embroidered bandana in remembrance of Flower of Love.

When his parents arranged a betrothal between Charles and a lovely Virginian heiress, he made no protest. Nothing mattered to him anymore. His world, his heart, was buried somewhere in China.

"Six weeks before the wedding," Grandfather concluded, "Charles, myself, and Charles's heiress were riding along this ravine by the light of the full moon. She was a blonde beauty and a bit of a coquette. Wishing to prove her power over her swain, she pointed to this pine tree, leaning so precariously over the deep ravine, and said, 'Climb this tree, Charles. I dare you!' And Charles did."

I sat up abruptly, staring wide-eyed at my Grandfather. "You mean the ghost of the falling man is my Uncle Charles?"

Grandfather nodded sadly. "I was there that night, when Charles climbed the tree. I saw the look on his face as he deliberately stepped on the rotten branch at the top. If you listen closely, you can hear his ghost calling his lover's name, Flower of Love, as he falls."

Elaine wept softly into Charlie's shoulder as he stroked her hair. I handed her the embroidered bandana, and she smiled at me through her tears.

"I thought *your* Charles should have a happy ending to his story," Grandfather said to my sister. He patted Elaine awkwardly on the shoulder and walked stiffly down the ravine path toward the house. I kissed her on the cheek and followed him, leaving the lovers alone in the light of a full moon.

10

Dead Man's Curve

I grew up hearing the stories about the phantom of Dead Man's Curve. All the kids told it at Scout Camp and at sleepover parties. According to the legend, a teenage boy picked up a girl who was walking beside the road near Dead Man's Curve. She was shivering with cold, so he gave her his jacket and then drove her home. It wasn't until he'd seen her to the door and driven away that he realized she still had his jacket. The next day he went to the house and rang the doorbell. An old woman answered the door and looked startled and then sad when the teenager asked after the girl. "That was my daughter who died in a car accident twenty years ago," the old woman told him. "Her ghost tries to come home on the anniversary of her death. She's buried in the churchyard next door." The old woman took the boy to the churchyard and pointed to a worn grave marker standing near the fence. Draped over the tombstone was the teenager's jacket.

"It's just an urban legend," my friend Bobby said at our lunch table a few weeks before our high school graduation. "The phantom hitchhiker is the most commonly told ghost story in America."

"It also happens to be a true story," his girlfriend, Jessica, said hotly. "It's that ghost that causes all those crashes at Dead

Man's Curve. When folks see her beside the road, they swerve to avoid her and smash into the brick wall. Sometimes their cars flip over the wall and roll down the mountain. That's what happened to Samantha and her boyfriend last year. Everyone says so."

Silence fell over the table, and everyone glanced at me. I swallowed hard and stared at my milk carton. Samantha's family lived next door to me, and I'd had a crush on her ever since I started noticing girls back in the sixth grade. I'd been green with jealousy when Samantha started going out with a senior from another high school. She was a beautiful blonde girl with dark-lashed gray eyes and a sweet smile for everyone she met. Everyone loved Samantha. A few days before her death, Samantha had been voted junior-class president. Her death was a shock to the whole community. The police thought her boyfriend had been drunk that night and caused the crash, but there wasn't enough left of either of them after the car fire to know for sure.

The bell rang, and everyone hurried to their next class. I dragged along behind, telling myself that grown men didn't cry. I shook my head, trying to clear it, but everywhere I looked that afternoon, I saw something that reminded me of Samantha. By the time the final bell rang, my mood was as black as the roiling thunder clouds overhead.

I was supposed to meet my girlfriend at the library to study for final exams, but I called to tell her I wasn't feeling well and was driving straight home, which was a lie. I wanted to drive up to the roadside memorial the senior class had put up near Dead Man's Curve in memory of Samantha. And I wanted to go alone.

The wind whipped against my black sports car as I drove up the mountain. Lightning crackled across the sky, and the whole world had a greenish tinge, so I turned on my headlights as I rounded the last bend and pulled off into a gravel parking area beside the small memorial grotto. The grotto was filled with statues of the Holy Family around a white cross that was nearly buried under flowers. Samantha's friends and family made sure there was always something decorating her memorial.

I shut off the engine and stepped out into the wind with a bunch of flowers in my hand. I placed them at the foot of the white cross and cried a little as the ozone grew thick around me. Lightning flashed, and I felt the electricity in the air as thunder cracked a few moments later. When raindrops started to fall, I ran hastily back to my car and flipped on the headlights. Time to go.

As the heavens opened above me and rain poured down in sheets, I turned the car around and started to drive carefully out of the parking area. I nearly ran down a white figure that was standing at the edge of the road. I blinked my eyes in amazement, recognizing Samantha. I'd know that face anywhere! Samantha was alive and well—not to mention soaking wet and waving for me to stop the car.

I skidded to a halt. "Samantha," I shouted as she pulled open the passenger door and jumped into the car. "You're alive," I said hoarsely, tears pouring down my face. Samantha's face was white as a sheet, and rain dripped from her clothes and honey-blonde hair.

"Take me home. I want to go home," Samantha said in a strained voice.

"Of course," I said, responding immediately to the urgency in her tone. I put on my right blinker, preparing to drive down the hill toward my house. Samantha grabbed my arm with an ice-cold hand and said, "Not that way. We have to go through Dead Man's Curve. I need to make it past the curve."

A shiver ran through my body at her words, and I glanced over at the girl seated beside me. In the dim twilight of the storm, her body glowed faintly and seemed to ripple under my glance. I turned my gaze back to the road, the blood running cold in my veins. Samantha wasn't alive after all. She was a ghost.

"Why do we need to drive through Dead Man's Curve?" I asked carefully, turning off my blinker and sitting very quietly in the driver's seat. An odd little bubble of time seemed to surround the two of us.

"I have to make it through Dead Man's Curve," Samantha repeated, her eyes glowing with white-hot tears. "I must make it through!"

"I think we should go home the regular way, Sam," I said, turning the wheel to the right.

"No!" the ghost screamed in fury. "No!" She pointed to the left, body pulsing with rage. Terrified, I turned left and headed slowly toward Dead Man's Curve in the pouring rain. Lightning flashed and thunder roared, but the storm held no terror for me now. All my attention was on the pulsing translucent figure in the car with me. The electric energy inside the car made my hair stand on end, and I was so cold my body shivered continuously.

"Drive faster," the ghost of Samantha commanded. "You are going too slow. We must make it through Dead Man's Curve."

I could see the curve about a hundred feet ahead of me, the low brick wall guarding the edge of a cliff on the left.

"I will not drive faster in this rain, Samantha. It isn't safe," I said, my voice high-pitched with fear.

"Why won't you listen to me, Charlie?" Samantha shouted. "You're drunk. You should let me drive. Give me the wheel!"

Charlie was the name of the boyfriend who had been driving the car in which they had been killed. A chill ran down my spine. "I'm not Charlie. I'm your next-door neighbor, Johnny," I said as calmly as I could.

Suddenly, translucent hands gripped the wheel beside mine, fighting me for control of the car. "Let go!" I screamed, trying to wrench the wheel away from the determined ghost. "Samantha, let go of the wheel!" My words came out as white puffs of steam in the frigid air. Wind whipped the inside of the car as it swerved drunkenly left, right, left as the ghost and I fought over the wheel.

"You will not kill me again, Charlie!" the phantom woman screamed in my ear. "Never again!"

The car slammed to the right so fast that I almost tilted out of my seat. We almost went into the woods to the right of the road.

"Let. Go," I roared, jerking the wheel violently to the left, my hands passing through the white translucent arms and torso of the ghost. The transparent flesh iced through my body as if I'd swallowed a cold smoothie too fast. My teeth started tingling.

The car lurched to the left as we reached Dead Man's Curve. My headlights picked up a red brick wall coming up too fast, far too close to my car.

"Nooooooo!" the phantom and I screamed together.

With a thundering crash, the screech of tearing metal, and the sound of shattering glass, the car hit the brick wall to the left of the curve. My head slammed against the back of the seat as

DEAD MAN'S CURVE

the engine burst right through the dashboard, driven backward by the unmoving wall, and the air bag exploded into my face. White-hot pain roared through my body in a blinding flash, and the world went black.

Days later, I came groggily awake inside a hospital room with my body encased in a cast, one leg extended upward in traction and more tubes and bags around me than one man should encounter in a lifetime. Brightly clad nurses in cheerful uniforms were busy around me, and a doctor in a mask was checking my IV.

Oh good, I'm alive, I thought wearily. Then the pain hit me, and I wished I wasn't.

All at once, a translucent white figure appeared directly above my bed. Her long, golden hair floated around her as if she was suspended in water and her white dress glowed from within.

"You killed me again, Charlie," the ghost howled, her lovely face twisted in fury. She reached straight down through cast and chest with her clawed fingers, grabbed my heart, and squeezed.

Try the Gingerbread

We arrived in Gettysburg just before dinner and unpacked our bags in the two-bedroom suite at our hotel. Karen, my sister, was scheduled to do a history tour with her college class, and I was along for the ride because I was a folklorist by trade and had never before visited the battlefield.

I had a good reason for this omission. Both my sister and I had a Sixth Sense, passed down through many generations in our psychically gifted Pennsylvania Dutch family. Whenever my sister and I traveled together, strange things happened—and that was when we visited normal places that weren't particularly haunted. Who knew what would happen when we visited a spook-strewn place like Gettysburg?

There was an air of tension in our suite as we debated where to go for dinner. In coming to Gettysburg, we had purposely entered one of the most haunted spots in the United States. Most folks visiting Gettysburg wondered *if* they were going to experience something supernatural during their visit; I just wondered *when* the spooky events would start. As it turned out, the answer was "right away."

We decided to visit the famous Dobbin House restaurant for dinner. Located in downtown Gettysburg, the Dobbin House is a Colonial restaurant with candlelit elegance, superior food, and gracious service that accurately reproduces the sights, sounds, and tastes of previous centuries. It is the oldest building in Gettysburg, located right across the street from the spot where Abraham Lincoln presented the Gettysburg Address. The historic house was a stopping point for slaves traveling the Underground Railroad. The slaves were concealed in secret hiding places located under the floors and in the walls. According to reviews we'd read about the restaurant, those hiding places could still be seen by guests.

I parked the car in the front parking lot, and we headed toward the restaurant entrance. Karen eyed the old house speculatively, already wondering if the alleged hauntings were accurate or only imagined. As soon as we stepped inside, we knew that the reports were spot-on. I felt a familiar chill across my skin, and I saw Karen blink rapidly as her extra sense came to life. I was rather envious of my sister's gift. She could look at a place and see it exactly as it appeared in the past. My own gift took the form of clairaudience—the ability to hear ghosts speaking.

The Colonial-garbed server suggested that we eat downstairs in the Springhouse Tavern, and we happily agreed. I fell in love with the tavern on my way down the period staircase with its worn boards, which groaned theatrically when we stepped on them. It was like walking into the past. My modern garb was out of place here. The dark, heavy beams on the ceiling; the stone walls; the brick floor; and the magnificent fireplaces were from another time altogether. The long wooden bar begged you to have a seat and take a drink while you waited for a table. It was one of the few times I hoped our table wouldn't be ready immediately, just so I could take in the atmosphere.

Karen hopped on a stool and ordered drinks for us. Meanwhile, I looked at the old spring and the dripping candles, stretching my Sixth Sense to the limit to see Who was here. I took a quick walk around the room before joining my sister at the bar. Chilly air swirled softly around my body, and I walked in and out of cold spots. Oh yes, this place was very haunted. According to the rumors, the ghosts of escaped slaves haunted the building, particularly this downstairs tavern, but the Person I was sensing had never been a slave. He was someone else. I wondered just Who he was. One thing was obvious: He was as curious about my sister and me as we were about him.

The hostess called us to our table before we finished our drinks, so we carried them with us to the far end of the room and slid into a booth. The candle on the table flickered merrily in the rush of moving air as we sat down and then burned straight and tall once we were settled in the booth. I eyed the shelf edging the wall beside us with interest. It was full of old-fashioned jugs, lamps, and other period items that added to the Colonial ambience around us. Then I grabbed a menu and read hungrily through the options.

As Karen and I debated the merits of various items, a cold spot descended upon our booth and settled on the shelf beside us. Abruptly, the candle streamed sideways as an ethereal breeze billowed from the shelf. My sister blinked in surprise and glanced at me over the top of her menu. I pinched my mouth in agreement and glanced at the candle. She nodded and returned to her perusal of the tavern specials as our server bustled up in her long skirt and white cap.

"And what will you ladies have?" she asked jovially.

We ordered hot sandwiches and then sipped our drinks as we chatted about our upcoming tour. Occasionally, one of us made oblique reference to the third Person at our table, but our server was bustling in and out with bread and drinks, and we couldn't speak freely with her present. The candle was rapidly developing a drip due to the steady, cool breeze coming from our Companion.

"Who do you suppose?" my sister said as she took a piece of bread and passed me the butter.

"I don't know," I replied. "Maybe the historical section on the menu will tell us something."

We munched bread and sipped wine as we read up on the history of the tavern. A paragraph in, we both spoke simultaneously: "Alexander Dobbin!"

And that's when my supernatural gift kicked in.

"*That's right*," said Alexander Dobbin—for my ears only—from his perch between us. My sister caught the look on my face and raised her eyebrows at me. But our server was back with our meals, so she dropped the matter in favor of food.

Our talk turned to the history tour, and Karen told me about her teacher and the classmates I would be meeting tomorrow. About halfway through our meal, the cold spot vanished and the candle flame burned upright without a flicker.

"He's gone," I told Karen.

She grinned and pointed over my shoulder. I turned and saw a crowded fireplace table with a wildly flickering candle. "He hasn't gone far," she replied.

While we studied the dessert menu, the cold spot returned. This time it settled on the seat beside me, between me and the wall shelf, causing the candle to flicker so wildly I thought

TRY THE GINGERBREAD

it would go out. I shivered, wishing I'd brought my jacket. Karen's eyebrows rose to her hairline as her Sixth Sense took in our returned Companion.

"Welcome back," I said politely to Dobbin and then turned my attention back to my sister. "So, Karen, what are you going to have for dessert?"

"I am going to have the chocolate brownie," she said.

"*Try the gingerbread,*" the ghost of Alexander Dobbin said with authority. I blinked in astonishment.

"The gingerbread?" I asked aloud. "Why should I try the gingerbread?"

"*Because it's very good here,*" Dobbin said. "*You will like it.*"

Karen was staring at me in glassy-eyed astonishment. "I beg your pardon?" she said, although she knew exactly to whom I spoke.

"Someone," I emphasized the word, "is recommending the gingerbread."

"Seriously?" my sister asked.

I grimaced wryly at her. Yes, seriously. She knew very well that my gift was clairaudience.

The server bustled up, all smiles, and asked for our dessert order.

"I'll have the fudge brownie with ice cream and chocolate sauce," my sister said.

"I hear your gingerbread is very good," I said with a glance toward the flickering candle. "I'd like to try it."

"*You won't be sorry,*" Dobbin said, his words landing in my inner ear at the same time my brain registered the server's reply.

Hush. I can't hear. I spoke silently to the ghost beside me. I felt him grin.

The gingerbread arrived. As predicted, it was very good, and it went very well with the Colonial atmosphere of the tavern.

"I still like chocolate better," I grumbled to the ghost after sampling a bite of my sister's dessert. Karen and Dobbin both grinned.

Our bill came and, with it, the end of our visit to the Springhouse Tavern of Dobbin House.

"We have to leave now," I murmured to Dobbin as Karen handed our payment to the server.

"*I know. Thank you for coming. Fare you well,*" Alexander Dobbin replied. The cold spot vanished from the table and the candle flame stood straight and tall once again. A few tables away, the candles started flickering wildly as a cold breeze blew over them.

Karen glanced at me, at our empty booth, and then at the neighboring tables. She rose with a smile. "Come on, let's go," she said and headed toward the staircase. I paused on the bottom step to look back at the tavern.

Good-bye, I called silently. Then I followed her up the stairs.

We exited into the darkness of a Gettysburg night to stroll around the various shops and get acquainted with the town. As we walked, I felt the air around me fill with a silent, electric charge as the spirits of Gettysburg awoke all along the main roads. It felt like the coming of a thunderstorm—a powerful concatenation of raw energies that might break over our heads at any time. As my sister chatted with a costumed guide waiting to give a ghost tour, I heard the staccato *rat-a-tat* of a drumbeat coming up the street. When we strolled onward toward the residential section a few blocks away, I walked headfirst into a cold wall of malevolent energy coming from a house on one

corner. I whirled crisply like a soldier on parade and walked back the way I came. Karen, a bold soul, asked me to wait while she crossed the street to investigate further. She barely got both feet planted on the far sidewalk when she hit the same invisible wall. She wheeled, bolted back across the street, and passed me at a swift trot. I joined her, hardly able to keep up. Neither of us felt like dealing with whatever lived in that house, not on our first night in town.

I hadn't minded the ghost in the tavern—old-fashioned, gruff gentleman that he was. But this overwhelming feeling of supernatural activity was too much on top of today's long drive. And we still hadn't made it to the battlefield. Enough was enough.

I turned to Karen and said, "I really can't deal with this now. Not after the long drive. I need to go back to the hotel and prepare myself for our visit to the battlefield tomorrow."

She took one look at my white face and agreed.

When I got back to my room, I firmly closed the curtains against the whistling soldiers marching past in the darkness and ignored the spirit that knocked for admittance on my wall.

So this is Gettysburg, I mused as I got ready for bed. *And we haven't even made it to the battlefield yet. I wonder what we will see tomorrow!*

Shaking my head in bemusement, I turned off the light and went to sleep.

12

The Noose

Salisbury was an overbearing man with a Puritan streak that did not allow room for laughing or dancing or leisure activities. As a prosperous landowner, he had many slaves and indentured servants working on his thousand-acre estate, and they were required to heed their master's every whim with instant obedience or risk severe discipline. It was a hard life.

It was certainly not the life Anna had envisioned when she signed her indenture papers in exchange for passage to America. The fun-loving girl grew up as a pampered only daughter in a village full of singing and laughter and parties. When a carriage accident killed both her parents, the orphaned Anna dreamed of a fine life in America and eagerly embarked on a trip to the New World. The stark reality of her new situation came as a shock to the merry girl. Life on the Salisbury estate was nothing but hard work and strict adherence to the master's laws. Her pretty dresses were replaced with sober clothing that adhered to the conventions of an indentured servant. She was reprimanded for laughing, for lingering in the kitchen to talk to the other servants, for singing while she worked, and for showing the master's children the latest dance steps.

The only pleasure Anna found in her new American life was in the company of the little farm dog who adopted her shortly after she arrived, and in her twice-a-day walks to the pasture to bring the cows in for milking. Anna loved the farm animals as passionately as she hated every other aspect of her American life. She named the little dog Rex and likewise assigned each milk cow a name based on its quirks and silly little habits. The cows came to the fence to greet Anna each morning and evening, as eager to see the merry girl as she was to see them. She sang to them in her mother tongue and would dance in the fields with her little dog. It was a small pleasure in her otherwise dull, work-oriented life.

About six months after Anna arrived in America, a new family moved into town. To Anna's delight, they came from the same part of Germany where she'd lived with her parents until the carriage accident. The Schumann family was every bit as warmhearted and merry and lively as Anna's parents had been—indeed, as every other family in her once-scorned and now dearly missed hometown had been. Anna snuck off to the Schumann home every chance she got. They always had guests over for dinner and dancing, and the young girl spent many evenings in this merry fashion after the other indentured servants had gone to bed.

All too soon, the other servants found out about Anna's innocent peccadilloes and reported her crimes to the overseer. Anna was summoned to the harsh presence of the master, and the Schumann family was forbidden to her. As punishment, she was set to the hardest, dirtiest tasks on the estate, under the strict supervision of a dour old maidservant who beat her whenever she paused for breath. Her little dog was taken away, and she was no longer allowed to fetch the cows for the morning and evening milking. Anna was miserable from sunup to sundown.

It seemed the last straw to the poor, overworked young girl when she heard that the entire village had been invited to a dance at the Schumann home and she would not be allowed to attend. Feeling angry and rebellious, Anna waited until the dour old maidservant fell asleep by the kitchen fire and snuck away to the party. The Schumanns welcomed her with glee, and soon she was dancing with the handsomest boy in the village. The farmhouse was filled with laughter and drinking and song, and Anna was the merriest of them all.

Anna was chuckling winsomely over something her new beau murmured into her ear when silence crept over the room like the coming of winter. Anna looked up and found herself staring into the eyes of Salisbury, the master of the estate, looming in the doorway of the farmhouse. The whole company, even the handsome young beau, backed away from the fury in his eyes, leaving Anna alone to face her master's wrath. He struck Anna's face twice with his riding whip, sending the stricken girl to her knees. Then he tied a length of rope around Anna's waist as if she were a rebellious beast and led her like a mule across the full length of the room, humiliating her in front of the gathered assembly. Anna's cheeks were scarlet with embarrassment as Salisbury jerked her through the front door and secured the rope to his horse's girth. It was only when Salisbury swung himself up in the saddle that Anna realized she would have to run behind the horse all the way back to the estate.

Aghast guests watched silently from the doorway and yard as Salisbury spurred his horse to a trot and Anna perforce trotted with it, stumbling and sobbing in terror and humiliation. She would never dare show her face in town again. The master could not have contrived a crueler punishment than this.

After running two miles down the moonlit road, Anna was gasping for breath. Tears pouring down her face, she begged the master to slow down. Instead, he spurred the horse to greater speed. Exhausted, Anna tripped and fell on her face in the muddy lane. The sudden tug on the girth frightened the horse. It reared with an anxious neigh and then bolted, throwing the master in the ditch and dragging the helpless Anna along behind, her body bouncing on every rock and log and fencepost on either side of the long lane. By the time Salisbury caught up with the fleeing horse, Anna was very gruesomely dead, her head held on by a single thread of skin and her face and body so torn up she was barely recognizable.

Salisbury was tried and convicted for the murder of the indentured Anna. But he was able to convince judge and jury that he had not intended the accident to happen, and so the judge decreed that Salisbury would not hang for his crime until he reached ninety-nine years of age. Not wishing to appear too lenient, the judge also ruled that Salisbury must wear a rope noose around his neck at all times.

The noose served as a continuous reminder of the estate owner's cruel deed, both to himself and others. The rough rope noose contrasted starkly with Salisbury fancy clothes and elegant manners. It instantly drew the eye. The servants and merchants who dealt with Salisbury every day found themselves speaking to the noose rather than to the man. People, even those who still did business with the convicted murderer, avoided Salisbury. The cruel master grew angrier and more forbidding with each passing day.

And then Anna returned. The first to see her were the milk cows she loved so dearly. They stampeded suddenly across the pasture one evening, crowding along the fence to peer at a white figure tied to a phantom horse that stumbled down the twilight lane. The cows mooed to their much-missed friend, but Anna's ghost raced away into the darkness without acknowledging her animal companions. The servant sent to bring the cows to the barn for milking ran away as frantically as Anna's ghost, terrified of what he had seen.

The little dog was the next to see Anna. It ran to meet an invisible presence at the gate and followed the nonperson all over the farm. The servants felt an ominous cold breeze whenever the dog drew near, and they cowered away as the ghost of Anna hurried past. Salisbury himself came face-to-face with the dog just before supper. The master gasped and backed away suddenly, staring into the empty air with his hands raised in defense. The overseer who attended his master saw nothing, but Salisbury cringed in terror, crying, "No, Anna." The noose around Salisbury's neck rose until the end was several feet above his head and Salisbury was dangling beneath it. The overseer grabbed his master's legs and held him up so he wouldn't choke to death. All at once, the rope was released with a malevolent chuckle and Salisbury and his overseer plunged to the ground. They lay panting with fear as the little dog barked merrily and circled them with its tail waving.

Shortly after this incident the Schumann family sold their farm and moved away, frightened by the apparition of a tied woman racing desperately across their yard and down the lane each night. No one in town would use the lane after dark for fear of encountering the ghost. Community opinion was so strongly against the master of the estate that Salisbury found it increasingly hard to do business in any of the surrounding towns. Angry citizens even spoke of tarring and feathering the master of the haunted estate and driving him out of the colony.

Desperate to foster some goodwill in the town, Salisbury threw a splendid dinner party for all the wealthy landowners in the region. Everyone who was anyone was invited, and most of those invited came to the party more out of curiosity than any feelings of goodwill toward their host. Salisbury stood in the main hall greeting his guests, dressed in his fine evening clothes with the noose tied loosely around his neck as if it were a cravat. The guests were embarrassed by the noose, and most averted their eyes when speaking to Salisbury.

The party was a flop from the first moment. No one laughed or joked over drinks, and the small talk during the awkward dinner was trivial indeed. More than one landowner gazed longingly out the windows and doorways, wishing the deadly dull evening would soon be over.

While dessert was served to the dinner guests, a huge gust of wind hit the mansion, shaking it from roof to wine cellar. A terrific banging sounded from the front hallway as the double doors of the stone mansion were torn from their hinges. The guests sprang to their feet as dead leaves and the stale smell of the grave swirled around the dining room. A great column of white light appeared in the doorway. Men in fancy suits scrambled away, and their jeweled ladies screamed and fainted as the light made its way through the center of the table, cutting along the length of the heavy oak furnishing like some massive white saw. The light stopped in front of Salisbury and grew larger, one end thrusting through the floorboards under the large table and the other end touching the ceiling. The table creaked as if under enormous pressure and then split in half. It fell to either

THE NOOSE

side of the shocked master with a crash of cutlery and silver plating, injuring those guests who had remained seated during the disturbance and splattering food and drink over the wiser guests who had fled to either side of the room.

Suddenly, the noose tightened around Salisbury's neck and he was yanked out of his chair, napkin still tucked into his collar. Salisbury was dragged—in the most humiliating fashion—across the room by the loose end of the noose. Before his terrified guests could blink, Salisbury was out the front door and running down the lane, each stride longer and more frantic than the last as the noose pulled tighter. Servants and guests raced out onto the moonlit lawn and saw a glowing phantom horse jogging down the lane with the master of Salisbury estate pulled along behind it. A translucent figure in a white dress sat in the saddle and urged the horse to go faster . . . *faster* with her spurs.

The bravest of the servants tried to follow their master but slammed right into an invisible wall that was as cold as ice and swirling with malignant fury. No one could pass through it. No one dared try. In the same moment that the glowing figures vanished into the distance, the invisible wall collapsed with a swooshing sound, blowing dust and debris into the faces of the hovering guests.

The bravest—and most curious—of the men followed the servants down the lane in search of the master. They found Salisbury's body two miles up the road, hanging by the neck from a tall oak tree. A small dog sat by his dangling feet, wagging its tail.

13

Ring around the Rosie

"Ring around the rosie, a pocket full of posies . . ."

I hear the voices chanting in the woods and look up from my lonely sandbox, enchanted by the sound. There are little girls and boys playing games in the forest behind my house. Someone to play with at last!

When we lived in an apartment in the city, there were lots of children that I could play with. But now we live in a brand-new house outside the city, and there are only grown-up neighbors on our block. There is no one to play with in my new home. I feel lonely all the time. So the sound of singing, laughing children is very welcome to me. I jump up and race into the woods, shouting, "Hello! Hello!" But no one answers me.

I hear the other children giggling just over the ridge and run up the hill as fast as I can. I get to the top in record time, but no one is there. Around me, the woods feel empty. I turn around, kicking dispiritedly at the autumn leaves underfoot, and wander down the hill to my backyard and the sad little toys in my lonely sandbox.

While I eat dinner with Mama and Papa, I hear the children singing from the woods behind my house: "Ring around the rosie, a pocket full of posies. Ashes, ashes, we all fall down!"

There is a dramatic thudding sound as several bodies tumble to the ground, and then giggles. I drop my chicken leg onto my plate and run to the window to look outside. All I see are trees. No children.

"Come back to the table, Sarah, and finish your dinner," Mama scolds.

"But I want to play with the children in the woods," I protest.

"What children in the woods?" Papa asks with interest.

"The ones who were singing just now," I say as I climb back into my chair, which is nearly too tall for me, and pick up my fried chicken with greasy fingers.

"No one was singing just now," Papa says, piling mashed potatoes onto his plate. "What an imagination the child has," he adds, grinning at Mama before putting a big spoonful of potatoes on my plate.

It is too dark to play outside when we finish supper, so I must wait until morning to look for the singing children.

I roam alone in the woods the next morning, listening for the sound of laughing voices. A new family must have moved into our neighborhood, I decide. A big family with many children. Their children are very shy. I hear them giggle and whisper words that I cannot make out. I run toward the sound, but they are too quick for me. It is like a game of hide-and-seek. "Ollie ollie oxen free!" I shout, jumping out from behind a big tree. But no one is there.

I hear the children laughing at me from the far side of the ridge, where the ground drops suddenly into a steep ravine. I am not allowed to play up there. Papa says it is too dangerous. I cannot follow the children up that hill. I cannot break my

RING AROUND THE ROSIE

promise to Papa. Sadly, I trudge away, going back to my lonely yard to play on the tire swing Papa tied to a tall tree.

At lunch I tell my mother about the game of hide-and-seek that the children are playing with me, but I know she doesn't believe me. She ruffles my hair and chuckles about my bright imagination. I find it odd that she cannot hear the children. They sing so loud: "Ring around the rosie, a pocket full of posies."

I ask Papa about the children when he gets home from work. He can't hear them either. He calls them my imaginary friends and says I will grow up to be a writer.

In the morning I wake to the sound of children's voices calling to me through the window. "Little girl, come and play," they sing over and over in my ears. The children sound like so much fun that I run outside as fast as I can to try to catch them. I plunge into the woods, calling back to the children, but no one answers. So I stand still as a mouse, trying to hear where they are hiding. Then I hear Mama calling from the house, "Sarah! Time for breakfast." As I hurry home, I hear giggles and the children start to sing: "Ring around the rosie, a pocket full of posies." Oh, why are they so shy?

It starts to rain after breakfast, so I stay inside putting a puzzle together in the living room while Mama has coffee with a neighbor lady.

"I wouldn't live here for any amount of money," the neighbor lady says to Mama. "The woods behind the house are haunted."

"Haunted?" Mama says in the bright tone she uses when she doesn't believe what someone is saying.

"Yes, haunted," the neighbor lady confirms. "Back in Colonial times, a local family was fleeing from the British when a Revolutionary battlefield swung too close to their farm. Bullets flew everywhere, and canons exploded all around. The father was wounded by a bullet, and the mother told her three children to flee into the woods while she followed with their injured father. The terrified children could barely see for all the smoke from the nearby canons. They fled to the top of the ridge, and the youngest slipped and fell into the ravine. The middle child stumbled and rolled after him, but the hem of her skirt was caught by her elder brother at the very edge of the ravine. Then the cloth ripped, and the little girl tumbled to her death in the stream far below. Her elder brother, making a last desperate grab for his sister, fell too and smashed onto the rocks between his two dead siblings. People say that the children's ghosts still roam the forest behind this house. They are lonely and often call to living children, asking them to come play with them. But this is a death summons. Any child who answers their call is doomed to die in the ravine as they did, for living children cannot play with ghosts."

"Hush," Mama says fiercely, looking around to see if I'd overheard this gruesome tale. "You will scare my daughter."

"Good," the neighbor lady replies unrepentantly. "Maybe she will stay out of the woods. They are not safe for a young child."

"You are talking complete nonsense," Mama says sharply. "Let's speak about something else." And she asks my neighbor if anyone in the area plays bridge.

I think about the neighbor's story while I finish my puzzle. She means well, but she obviously doesn't know what she is talking about, I decide. The children in the woods are real people. They laugh and sing and dance. Ghosts don't laugh and sing. Ghosts are scary creatures. They would never play Ring around the Rosie.

While I am eating my breakfast the next morning, I hear the children call to me from the woods. "Sarah, come out and play," they cry. They know my name! Now that we are introduced, they will have to let me play with them. I finish my breakfast so fast that the milk spills from my cereal bowl. Then I run outside with my blue smock still dripping wet.

"Where are you?" I call as I run into the woods. I hear them giggling. Their footsteps scamper first here, then there. I laugh aloud and follow them uphill and down. They are always just out of sight. Then they start singing somewhere near the top of the forbidden ridge, "Ring around the rosie, a pocket full of posies!" I race up the hill and careen down the far side. At last I see them! The children are right in front of me, dancing in a circle on the edge of the ridge. Their clothing looks a bit strange and their bodies flicker around the edges, but I am too busy running to notice.

Then my foot slips in the loose dirt and I slide down the hill on my bottom. I am going very fast, too fast. The ravine is directly in front of me, and I can see black cliffs with jagged outcroppings like sharp teeth. If I tumble over the edge, there is a steep drop of a hundred feet onto hard, sharp rocks in the water of the stream far below.

I scream and call to the children for help. They are still dancing in a circle, singing, "Ring around the rosie, a pocket full of posies." I don't think they can hear me. I am sliding faster and faster down the slope, banging painfully against rocks and vainly trying to grab roots—anything to stop my fall. My heart pounds with fear, and I am sweating and cold by turns.

"Help me," I scream as my body pitches off the edge of the cliff. For a moment, I hang in the air above the ravine like a floating feather. Ice-cold bands close around my chest as I realize that the children are dancing in a circle in midair, far above the rocky floor of the ravine. As I plummet through the middle of their game, their ice-cold bodies chill my skin. I scream and fall for a long, long time. For the rest of my too-short life. Above me, the children's voices are still singing, "Ring around the rosie."

PART 2

Powers of Darkness and Light

14

$\mathcal{N}ine\ \mathcal{E}leven$

As a special treat for our twentieth anniversary, we decided to take the sunset cruise around lower Manhattan the Sunday before Labor Day. It was a silly thing to do—totally tourist—but sometimes playing tourist is fun, even for someone living and working daily in the shadow of the Big Apple. My husband took me out for a fancy lunch at a restaurant near the South Street Seaport, and we lingered over linguine for more than an hour before the boarding call came.

The ship was packed with tourists from all nations, wearing sunglasses and laughing in half a dozen languages. But the smiles and gestures were universal. Everyone was amazed by the Statue of Liberty and Ellis Island, and by the glow of the sunlight on the towering New York skyline.

My husband nipped down to the concessionaire and returned with two cups of hot chocolate, just perfect for sipping in the cool breeze that whipped around us as the boat moved through the choppy water.

My husband was all over the place with his digital camera, taking photos of everything from a seagull perched cheekily on a rotting dock to the grinning tour guide as he pointed out the sights. Finding me leaning against a rail, watching lower

NINE ELEVEN

Manhattan glow with golden light as the sun set in the west, he took my hand and gave me a kiss. "Happy twentieth anniversary, sweetheart," he murmured in my ear and gave me a tickle and a squeeze. I squealed like a teenager and then hugged him back. He put his camera away, and we stood watching as dusk crept over the city and one by one the lights came on. That was glorious too.

We were on the East River now, between Brooklyn and lower Manhattan. Muttering something about catching the reflections on the water, my husband grabbed his camera and hastened to the front of the boat. I watched him go with a grin. Twenty years of marriage had hardly changed him! Well, five minutes of romance was better than none, I decided with a shake of my head and a fond smile.

I returned my gaze to the beautiful glow of the World Trade Center, its twin towers looming over the rest of the city like matching sentinels. Then I blinked suddenly in surprise as the whole world shivered around me. A keening noise sounded in my ears, as if a high-pitched alarm was going off or someone was blowing a dog whistle. The air started to shimmer before my eyes, like heat rising from pavement. And then I was looking at the harsh white light of midmorning in New York City and, before me, the silhouette of a large jet airliner was flying straight toward the North Tower of the World Trade Center! I gasped and shouted an idiotic warning to the pilot, who could not possibly have heard me from a boat on the East River. My garbled words came out as a tiny squeak, which was lost immediately in the wind. A moment later, the airplane intersected with the tower and disappeared.

My heart was pounding painfully against my ribs as I leaned hard against the rail, hyperventilating in alarm. My hands gripped the bar so hard that my knuckles were white with the strain. What had just happened? Knees trembling, I stared in shock as morning sunshine lit the World Trade Center, wondering where the airplane had gone. Had the pilot swerved at the last minute?

Suddenly, a second silhouette—also of a large airplane—appeared from the opposite direction and flew straight toward the South Tower. I thought I would faint as it intersected with the shimmering building and vanished. The keening sound rose higher in pitch until my ears burned with it, and tears sprang to my eyes. Goose bumps covered my whole body as the air twisted and writhed around me. For a moment, I smelled smoke and heard screams. A tight, too-calm voice said, "Nine eleven. Nine eleven." It sounded like a cry for help. Or a prayer.

Yes, I thought fuzzily, *someone should call 9-1-1.* If ever there was an emergency, this was it.

And then the world shuddered back into its proper place. I was staring at two glowing towers in the gentle light of sunset, and the voices of happy tourists murmured all around me. A young couple turned to me with excited smiles and asked me to take their picture with the World Trade Center in the background. I accepted the camera with shaking hands and had difficulty lining up the shot for them. I kept expecting the silhouetted airplanes to fly into the towers and ruin the picture. I was certain the tourists would find the pictures too blurry to keep when they reviewed them later.

I was still shivering when my husband returned and casually slung his arm around me. Turning away from the magnificent glitter of lights on the horizon, he asked: "Are you cold, honey? Do you need your sweater?"

"I'm fine," I said shortly, not wanting to explain the strange vision I'd seen. I couldn't understand it, and I didn't want to think about it.

"Wow, look at that," my husband cried, pointing upriver. Thrusting away the strange appearance of two silhouetted planes flying right into the twin towers, I obediently gazed upriver and drifted back into tourist mode.

A few days later, I was vacuuming the living room after breakfast when the phone rang. It was my husband, calling from his office in midtown Manhattan. "Turn on the television right now," he said, knowing I rarely watched TV in the morning. His voice sounded strange. I grabbed the remote control and switched on the television. Immediately, the screen was filled with a picture of the World Trade Center towers, black smoke billowing up around them.

"Two planes just hit the towers," my husband said, as the newscaster's voice told me the same thing. "I can see the smoke from my office window!"

I gasped in shock, my heart seeming to pause inside my chest, and I nearly dropped the phone. Two airplanes . . .

Oh . . . my . . . God!

Two airplanes had hit the twin towers.

I fell to my knees, body shaking so hard I couldn't stand. I heard my husband's voice in the phone. It sounded a long way off, as if he lived on another planet.

"Honey, did you hear me? Honey?"

Hearing alarm in his voice, I put the receiver to my mouth and gasped, "I heard you. I'm watching it now."

I put the phone back down, just as the scene on the TV cut to a clipping of the second plane hitting the South Tower. I shut my eyes in extreme mental agony. It was exactly the scene I'd seen in silhouette during our Labor Day cruise around New York City.

My husband was talking again. I opened my eyes and tried to pick up the phone. It kept slipping out of my sweating hands. After three tries, I leaned down and spoke into it, reassuring him that I was all right—at least physically.

We stayed on the phone together, watching our separate newscasts as rescuers tried to get to the people trapped on the upper floors of the two burning towers, listening to panicked newscasters speculating as to the cause of the disaster.

My husband and his colleagues had gathered in a meeting room with a window overlooking downtown Manhattan. They were simultaneously watching the newscast on television and looking out the window at the chaotic scene. I could hear bits and pieces of their commentary as I stared at my own TV screen. Once, I heard my husband exclaim in horror as he witnessed several people throw themselves off the top of the twin towers to avoid burning to death in the fire that encased the upper floors.

There came an unexpected rumbling sound. People began screaming and shouting on the television as first one and then the second tower collapsed before my stunned gaze. My heart squeezed with pain. *What about all those people trapped inside?* I thought in horror. I realized that I had just seen hundreds of real people with real lives die in an instant.

My stomach roiled. I ran for the bathroom and was sick into the toilet. Twice. I sat beside the bowl, panting and wiping the sour taste from my mouth, too sick to stand up. I was horrified beyond even tears, my body shaking. *Dear God,* I prayed, and stopped, not knowing what else to say.

Suddenly, I flashed back to my Labor Day vision. Oh, my gosh—had my vision somehow caused this? My body shuddered in fearful reaction to the thought. But no—how could it? I'd seen a vision of this disaster, what my Nova Scotian grandmother called a forerunner. But I'd never heard of visions *creating* disasters. I hoped.

This is not your fault, I told myself firmly.

I hauled myself upright, using the toilet as a crutch. I rinsed the bitter taste from my mouth and brushed my teeth. Then I walked shakily to the living room, one hand on the wall for support, and sat down on the couch to watch events unfold in New York City, my mind stunned into a strange stillness that was probably shock. A small voice in the back of my brain started speculating on how many of my friends—or my friends' friends—worked in the World Trade Center. And how many of them had made it out alive.

I don't know how long I sat on the couch, unable to move, unable to look away from the chaos I saw on the TV screen. My thoughts came slowly, one at a time, as if they were swimming through cold molasses. Where would these terrible events take us as a nation? This day felt momentous, life-changing in some negative way.

What day is it, anyway? I wondered abruptly. As if in answer, I heard the newscaster say in a tight, too-calm voice, "We will never forget the events of this day, September 11, 2001."

I took a deep breath and burst into tears. It was September 11. Nine eleven.

15

El Blanco

Royal Lane was the only road that led between the ranch where Ted worked as a wrangler and Sylvie's hometown, which was why he'd grown so familiar with Royal Lane of late. Ted had met Sylvie at one of the town's infrequent dances and fallen head over heels for the pretty maiden with red curls and an impish smile. Sylvie was a Harvey Girl, working as a waitress in one of the restaurants Fred Harvey had set up along the major railways in the Southwest. The ranch manager had been sympathetic to Ted's cause and had given his head wrangler time off to court the lovely Harvey Girl. Ted had ridden into town today with a ring burning a hole in his pocket, and Sylvie had made him the happiest of men when she'd accepted it and his marriage proposal. They'd hurried next door to the church to ask the priest if he'd read the banns and marry them next month when Ted returned from taking the ranch cattle to market. The priest said he'd be delighted.

What with one thing and another, Ted was late setting out for the ranch. Sylvie had begged him to spend the night in town and return home in the morning, but he was scheduled to move a herd of cattle to market early the next day and couldn't stay. He felt Sylvie's anxious gaze watching him as he headed out of town and down Royal Lane. Though she hadn't said anything, Ted knew she was afraid that he would meet El Blanco somewhere out on the trail.

El Blanco was the name of the phantom that folks claimed haunted the river ford on Royal Lane. It was said that El Blanco was the angry spirit of a train robber who was killed in a flash flood while escaping from a posse. The ghost tried to kill anyone crossing the ford at dusk, believing them to be part of the posse that had driven him into the canyon to die.

Ted had heard stories of cowboys who traveled down the canyon road at dusk and never returned. A couple of times over the past year, men had come riding hell-for-leather into town and raced into one of the taverns, claiming that El Blanco had grabbed their horses' bridles and tried to pull them into the river. Most folks reckoned the stories were just hokum; flash floods and river mist would explain them all. People largely disregarded the tale, though it was repeated frequently enough to become part of the local color.

Ted's thoughts were on his bride-to-be as he rode deeper into the twilight canyon, kept company by the rustle of small creatures settling in for the night and the *clip-clop* of his horse's hooves. It wasn't until he was almost at the bottom, where the trees grew thicker and the sound of flowing water filled the canyon, that Ted remembered the story of El Blanco. He grinned to himself as a chilly breeze swept over the river and blew under his wide-brimmed hat. He'd have to make up some spooky tale about the ghost and use it to scare the other cowboys when he got back to the ranch.

He chuckled aloud at the thought as his horse ambled past the last tree on the bank and stepped into the water. In that instant, a white figure leapt into the river beside Ted and grabbed his horse's bridle in one glowing hand. The horse screamed and reared. Ted fought for balance as the white figure tugged on his horse's mouth. The gelding lashed out at the glowing form with his front hooves. They passed through the man's glowing body without connecting with flesh. As the horse's hooves reconnected with the stones of the riverbed, Ted drew his pistol and shot several bullets into the shimmering figure holding the bridle. It didn't flinch.

Ted fought desperately to stay on the bucking horse. He didn't want to know what would become of him if he fell into the river at the feet of the phantom. Shivers ran through Ted's straining body as he stared into the glowing red eyes of El Blanco over the head of the thrashing gelding. In life, El Blanco had been a tall man dressed as a cowboy with a thief's black bandana tied over his mouth and nose. In death, he wore the same clothes, but his phantom body stretched and twisted in unnatural ways, easily following the twists and turns of Ted's panicked gelding without letting go. His arms seemed to tie themselves into knots and weave impossibly around each other until the sight made Ted dizzy.

The phantom was pulling them deeper into the river, toward a fast section of water a little south of the ford. If the phantom dragged them under the deep water, Ted knew he and his horse were dead.

"Let go of my horse!" Ted screamed in panic, emptying the last of his bullets into the phantom. When that didn't work, he dropped the gun in frustration and pulled his knife from his boot. It was a family heirloom said to protect the wearer against evil. Praying that this was the truth and not just another tall tale,

EL BLANCO

Ted leaned over the straining gelding's neck and slashed the knife through the misty white forearm of the ghost. The ghost screamed when the metal touched its translucent flesh, and it vanished with a popping sound, leaving a glowing hand still attached to the horse's bridle. The horse screamed and whirled, running back the way it had come. Ted hung on for dear life as the horse scrambled up the bank and bolted along the trail, ghostly hand flapping wildly against its shoulder.

They made the two-mile ride from the twilight ford to the town in record time. Folks spilled out into the darkened street with lanterns and torches when they heard thundering hooves approaching at full speed. Ted rode up the main street on his frantic horse, screaming desperately for the priest. When the townsfolk saw the ghost hand grasping his bridle, they started screaming too.

Ted hauled on the reins and managed to halt his exhausted horse by the church steps. As he slid off the trembling beast, the phantom hand let go of the bridle and fastened itself around Ted's neck, gripping so tightly it cut off his breath. Ted staggered around in panic, trying to remove the ghost's hand before it killed him. He heard Sylvie's voice desperately crying his name as the priest threw a glass of holy water over his head. The ghost hand sizzled and burned away, freeing Ted's throat moments before he blacked out.

When Ted came to a moment later, he was lying on the ground in Sylvie's arms while the priest and the doctor tended to the burning red marks on his throat, left by the evil hand of El Blanco.

"How did you manage to escape the ghost?" the priest asked the cowboy when the doctor finished dressing the wound.

"I cut off his hand with my knife," Ted explained, handing the blade to the priest. "It was my grandfather's knife. It's been handed down in my family for many generations. My grandfather told me it was good protection against evil."

The priest examined the blade, and then smiled. He pointed to several symbols carved into the handle. "This knife has been blessed by a saint," he said. "No wonder it worked against the ghost. You are a very lucky man."

"Yeah," Ted agreed shakily, accepting his blade back and clutching his bride-to-be close. "I sure am."

16

The Old Trunk

The couple lived in a two-story log cabin at the edge of a lovely lake just outside town. The man was a farmer—of sorts—with a plain-faced, industrious wife who milked the cows, swept the barn, fed the hens, and did the work of ten. As for the farmer, well, he preferred sitting by the lake with his pipe or talking to the fellows in the mercantile in town. Sometimes, when the mood struck, he'd hitch his horse to the old broken-down plow and turn over the soil in one of his fields, but in truth, he never got much accomplished. It was the wife's industry that kept food on the table and the beef cattle fed.

Because her lazy husband was also a spendthrift, the industrious wife saved every dollar she made and hid money all over the house. She accumulated a large secret stash over several years of marriage, and her husband—though sometimes indignant over her prudent measures—was too lazy to search for the cash.

One day the industrious wife received a telegram from her sister, begging her to come east to see their dying mother. The wife left at once, leaving her husband in charge of the lakeside farm. After lazing about for a week, the indolent farmer went to town and picked up a scarlet lady from the red-light district. He brought his new girlfriend home to the farm, and they caroused by the lake at night and spent most of the day sleeping.

"You should try to find my wife's hidden cash," the farmer told his girlfriend. "She's got a decent amount stashed away somewhere. If you find the money, I could get rid of my wife and we could live it up in style."

Now, the new girlfriend was just as lazy as the farmer. But she liked the idea of living in a pretty cabin on a lake, so she poked around the house a bit, finding some cash in the cookie jar and some hidden under a glass figurine on the mantel. The girlfriend never put anything back once she moved it, so odds and ends began accumulating on tables and chairs as she searched for the money.

"Honestly, I'm better off keeping my wife instead of you," criticized the farmer when he came into the cabin and saw the mess. "At least she keeps the house clean."

"But look at all the money I found," the girlfriend said, waving a wad of cash at him. "Enough to keep us in style for a month!"

"My wife's got fifty times that much money hidden somewhere," said the farmer, but he didn't put much heart into it. He liked his new girlfriend better than his wife. "You better keep looking. My wife's coming home tomorrow, and if you don't find that money, you'll have to leave."

The girlfriend spent the rest of the day searching the house and the barn. She pried up floorboards and combed through the attic, but she didn't find anything.

"Look," she said to the farmer the next morning. "We've got enough to live on for a month. If you get rid of your wife when she comes home today, we'll have plenty of time to find the rest of the money."

The farmer grumbled a bit but finally agreed. When his wife drove into the yard, he hid behind the front door with a hatchet. As soon as she stepped into the house, he killed her with one mighty blow, nearly decapitating her. The poor wife never knew what hit her.

The farmer threw the body into a moldy old trunk his wife kept at the foot of their bed and then cleaned the blood off the axe and the parlor floor. That night, under the light of a full moon, the farmer rowed out into the lake and pitched the old trunk overboard. Unaccustomed to so much labor, the farmer rowed home exhausted and in a bit of a rage. *I should have made my girlfriend dump the body,* he fumed to himself. After all, he was doing her a favor by letting her live in his house.

The farmer was eager for a big breakfast when he woke in the morning. Every morning, his wife used to make him ham and eggs with toast and fresh-churned butter and some strong coffee. That's what he needed this morning after all his labors yesterday. His wife always made him wonderful breakfasts, and he was sure his pretty new girlfriend would do the job twice as well.

The farmer ambled into the kitchen and found his girlfriend eating the last slice from a loaf of bread. "Make me some breakfast," he commanded, citing his desired menu. The girlfriend laughed in the farmer's face. "Make your own breakfast, you lazy sod. I already made mine!" She sauntered out of the room, leaving the flummoxed farmer to fend for himself.

"And clean up this mess," he shouted after her. "The house looks like a pigsty after all your searching yesterday."

"Clean it up yourself. I'm going back to bed," the girlfriend shouted back.

The farmer stood in the kitchen staring angrily at the mess, realizing he'd just murdered a perfectly good wife in exchange for this saucy girlfriend who was too lazy to cook him breakfast. This did not bode well.

For the next three weeks, the lazy girlfriend spent her days eating and sleeping as the house grew messier and the cash ran low. The farmer was forced to shop for his own groceries and cook their meals so they wouldn't starve. And he had to search for his dead wife's secret cash stores himself, because his new girlfriend refused to lift a finger to help. By the end of the month, the house smelled to high heaven, the farmer had no clean clothes left, and they were down to a few measly dollars in cash. The farmer was desperate. If he didn't find the money soon, he'd have to go to work—and he hated work even more than he hated the mess.

That night, the farmer and his girlfriend argued over the missing money and the dirty house. The farmer threatened to throw the girlfriend out, and she threatened to turn him in to the authorities for murdering his wife. That threat shut him up good. The farmer stalked to his chair on the porch and glared out over the lake, too riled up to sleep.

It was a clear night with a full moon, the same kind of night on which he'd rowed out into the lake to dump the body of his murdered wife. The farmer brooded on this foolish behavior. He didn't miss his wife as a person, but he missed the comfortable lifestyle he'd thrown away in favor of a pretty face. And now he was miserable. He glared at the lake, consumed with self-pity.

Around him, the night stilled. The wind died away, the crickets ceased to chirp, and the night birds fled to their nests. As the air grew sharp and cold, tiny sounds became magnified out of proportion in the intense silence. The farmer could hear each tiny pop as small bubbles floated from the bottom of the lake and burst on top of the glittering waves. The popping sound filled his ears until it dominated his world, and he knew that something dark and twisted was rising from the dark depths.

The farmer sat frozen in his chair, unable to move. Every nerve tingled with dread as a dripping, slime-encrusted corpse broke through the black water's surface and moved inexorably toward shore. Each sloshing footstep drove a spike of terror down his spine. His rotting wife had risen from the lake, and he was helpless to flee, tied to the chair with bands of ice that gripped his arms and turned his legs to jelly. The acrid smell of swamp gases and decay flooded the farmer's nostrils as the misshapen form gurgled its way out of the water and across the short strip of land that separated lake and porch.

When the creature reached the porch stairs, it lifted rotting weeds from its bloated face and leered up at the farmer. He cowered away with his hands over his face as the corpse gave a hissing laugh, black spores and weeds shooting from its swollen lips like spittle.

"Don't worry, husband, I am not here to kill you, in spite of what you did to me," the desiccated creature bubbled. "I am here to help you get rid of that useless scarlet woman living in my house. There's rat poison in the cupboard under the sink. If you put it into your girlfriend's coffee tomorrow morning, I will tell you where I hid my money."

The farmer gasped in excitement when he heard this promise. He peeked at the corpse between his shaking fingers and saw it grinning up at him through rotting teeth. Its cold, decaying breath filled the air of the porch; the smell making

THE OLD TRUNK

his stomach roil and his skin crawl. Unable to bear the corpse's proximity, the farmer shut his eyes once more. After an endless, horrible moment, he heard its sloshing footfalls retreat from the porch. When he heard a massive splash, the farmer opened his eyes and saw the corpse sinking down under the glittering waves of the lake.

The farmer reeled into the cabin, legs shaking so badly he could hardly stand. But his mind was elated. His dead wife was so perceptive. It was obvious, now that he came to think on it, that he had been led astray by a fallen woman. The murder was entirely the fault of his girlfriend, and it was his solemn duty to rid the world of such an evil woman. The farmer's just reward for such a deed would be riches and freedom. The farmer crawled into bed beside his fallen woman and fell asleep with a smile on his lips.

When the farmer woke in the morning, the floor was covered with wet footprints and a large puddle of water stood at the side of the bed. "Where did this mess come from?" he asked his girlfriend grumpily.

"Maybe it rained in the night and the roof leaked," she said evasively, not meeting his gaze. The girlfriend flounced out of bed and went to the kitchen to get something to eat.

"The lazy wretch spilled the water from the washbasin and didn't bother to clean it up," the farmer growled as he jumped over the cold puddle, trying to reach his clothes without getting his feet wet.

Still, he reflected, it was the last mess his girlfriend would ever make in this house. The thought cheered him. He just had to make some poisoned coffee, and his problems would melt away like snow.

The farmer whistled jauntily as he dressed and made his way to the kitchen. To his surprise, a fresh-brewed pot sat on the table, and his girlfriend was stirring sugar into a full cup as he entered the room.

"Let's not argue today," she said winsomely. "See, I've turned over a new leaf. Here's fresh coffee for you, and I may even cook us some breakfast." She placed the mug before him and then poured herself a cup.

"Do we have enough eggs?" the farmer asked cunningly.

"Let me check," his girlfriend said and stepped into the pantry to get the egg bowl.

Quick as a wink, the farmer opened the cupboard door, flicked the rat poison out from under the sink, and dropped a couple of heaping teaspoons into his girlfriend's cup. By the time she returned with the eggs, he was buttering some bread and drinking his coffee. His girlfriend set the eggs on the stove to boil and then sat down and drank her own cup, watching the farmer as closely as he watched her.

As their meal drew to a close, the farmer realized he was feeling queasy and his skin felt cold and clammy. And his girlfriend still looked healthy as a horse. Darn it. He thought he'd put enough poison into her cup. Maybe two teaspoons wasn't enough.

The farmer swayed a bit and had to clutch the back of the chair when he stood. "I'm feeling a might poorly," he said to his watching girlfriend.

A huge grin broke over her face. "Good," she said.

"What do you mean good?" he asked suspiciously.

"I mean good. That means the rat poison is working!"

"Poison," he gasped, glaring at her through tearing eyes.

"Yes, poison. Your wife's corpse came to our room last night and told me she'd reveal the whereabouts of her secret hoard of cash to me if I poisoned your coffee this morning," his girlfriend said triumphantly. Then she clapped a hand to her mouth, looking chagrined, and raced to the sink to be sick.

The farmer clutched desperately at his cramping stomach and cried, "But my wife came to me last night and promised to give me the money if I poisoned you!"

The girlfriend turned from the sink, wiping her mouth. "You poisoned me too?" she shrieked as sweat beaded her forehead.

The kitchen door burst open with a bang, and a cold breeze swept the smell of swamp gas and decay through the room. Slurping wet footsteps groaned across the porch as the swollen, rotting figure of the murdered wife dripped into the kitchen. At the sight of the sick couple, she bubbled a laugh that shook the rafters of the cabin and caused chinking to fall from between the logs. "You poisoned each other," she cried gleefully. "Just as I asked."

The girlfriend sank to the floor beside her paramour, gasping, "You double-crossed us!"

"Not at all. I intend to show you where the money is hidden," the desiccated corpse hissed with glee. It pointed to the kitchen doorway and a dripping wet, water-filled trunk appeared. It was the same old trunk in which the farmer had bundled his murdered wife's body a month ago, the one he had thrown into the lake.

"The money is hidden in the lining of my old trunk," the phantom said triumphantly. It swept a swollen hand along the lid of the trunk, tearing out the moldy, water-soaked lining. Packet upon packet of wet, decaying money fell into the water and bobbed gently inside the trunk. It was more money than the dying couple had ever seen—more than they could have spent in a lifetime. Especially their current lifetime, which would end in about ten minutes.

The specter laughed, causing a large portion of the cabin roof to cave in. Then the rotting corpse vanished, taking the trunk of money with it and leaving the dying farmer and his girlfriend writhing in agony on the kitchen floor.

Collateral

Jerry was a flibbertigibbet when it came to money. Even his new bride, Virginia—who still had stars in her eyes over her boyish-faced husband—had to admit the truth of this statement. It worried her now and then, especially when Jerry—who was a collector of useless items—bounced through the front door of their apartment with some new purchase of little artistic merit and dubious value instead of the item he'd been sent to procure. Currently, their new apartment was furnished with an old-fashioned butter churn, two spinning wheels, several barn decorations, a cowbell, and two collections of chipped china. What the apartment did *not* possess was furniture. Jerry had sacrificed this basic need in favor of his antiques mania.

Virginia sighed a little, looking over her crowded front room. A time was coming in the not-so-distant future when she would have to put her foot down and take over the family finances. But not yet. Let Jerry have his fun. They had the rest of their lives to live on a budget.

Virginia pulled up a footstool, the only item that vaguely resembled a chair, and started balancing the checkbook on the seat of one of the spinning wheels. After a time, she heard footsteps trudging up the stairs. She frowned. That couldn't be Jerry, who went everywhere at a cheerful trot. Who could be calling so close to dinner? Then she heard a key in the front lock and knew it must be Jerry. Virginia rose from the stool and hurried into the tiny front hallway, worried that he might be ill.

Jerry stood in the doorway, tragedy written all over his handsome, boyish face. Virginia flew to his side. "Darling, what is wrong?" she cried.

"I've lost it," he said numbly. "I've lost the rent money."

"You can't have lost it," said Virginia. "It's right here in the bank." She waved the checkbook, which she still clutched, for emphasis.

"No. I took it out yesterday," Jerry said. "There was an antique car for sale in the used-car lot. A real beauty!" His face glowed with sudden excitement. "I was going to put a down-payment on the car, and then Harry called and told me about this sure winner at the horse races, so I put the money down on Little Bit instead."

"I gather Little Bit lost the race?" Virginia asked grimly.

"Yes," Jerry said glumly, sinking down onto a bench that encircled the huge hat rack he'd brought home last week. "And my next paycheck doesn't arrive until next Thursday."

And the rent was due tomorrow. Virginia didn't say it aloud.

"What are we going to do?" she asked.

"I asked around at the Russian grocery store on the corner," Jerry replied. "There's a fellow named Vladimir who lives over the grocery. Apparently, he loans money to folks in difficulties to help tide them over. I was thinking of stopping by to see him."

A fellow who loaned money to people in difficulties. Virginia didn't have any trouble interpreting this vague statement. Vladimir was obviously a loan shark who preyed on people when they were down and out. Like them.

"I don't see what else we can do," Jerry said. "Once my paycheck arrives we can pay him back."

"That check is already earmarked for other expenses," Virginia said carefully. "Food, for one. We can't afford to pay high interest on a short-term loan."

"I don't think we have a choice," said Jerry, keeping his eyes firmly fixed on the antique mirror gracing the wall so he wouldn't have to look at his wife.

Virginia sighed and said, "All right. I will go get my coat."

Jerry turned in surprise. "You don't have to come, darling."

"Oh yes, I do," Virginia said grimly, grabbing her coat from the front closet.

The couple hurried down the block to the Russian grocery. Olga, the wife of the proprietor, was stacking tomatoes into a bin when they arrived. Jerry asked her if they could see Vladimir. Olga's eyes widened and she put her basket down with a thump. "You do not want to see Vladimir," she said, waving agitated hands for emphasis. "He will bleed you dry."

"I am afraid we must," said Jerry. "We will lose our apartment if we are late with our rent. It's written into our contract. How do we get to Vladimir's place?"

Reluctantly, Olga showed the couple to a steep staircase half hidden behind a shelf full of canned sauerkraut. "Be cautious, my dear," she whispered, clutching Virginia's arm as Jerry bounded up the stairs. "Vladimir will bleed you dry if you do not take care."

COLLATERAL

Virginia patted the plump hand and extracted herself. *This Vladimir must live in squalor,* she mused, staring in distaste at the water-stained wallpaper as she followed her husband up the dingy steps.

Jerry knocked on the door at the top of the stairs, and a plummy voice that fairly breathed sophistication and wealth bade them enter. Virginia's eyes widened. This was not the voice she was expecting to hear at the top of such a pokey little staircase.

Virginia's surprise increased as they stepped through the door. The apartment was filled with lovely carved furnishings made of dark red wood. Velvet draperies in rich crimson hues hung at the windows, and red sofas stood on either side of a deep fireplace. Candles stood on every available surface, lending a romantic air to the room. A refined gentleman in a dinner jacket was pouring himself a glass of wine from a decanter on a cherry side table.

"Are you Mr. Vladimir?" Jerry asked as Virginia gazed around her yearningly. Their antiques-strewn apartment was nothing like this elegant abode. And Jerry looked like a little boy beside this handsome stranger.

"Just Vladimir," the elegant man said. He gave Virginia a piercing glance that—despite its brief duration—took in every aspect of her lovely person. Then he turned his attention to Jerry and bade him take a seat on the sofa. For Virginia, he pulled up a lovely upholstered armchair and then sat down beside her.

"What can I do for you?" Vladimir said to Jerry.

"I need to borrow some money," Jerry said. And then he blurted out the embarrassing details.

Virginia's face went wooden as she tried to suppress her emotions. Vladimir gave her a sidelong glance, his thin mouth twitching in sympathy. When Jerry finally wound down, Vladimir explained his terms. The interest rate was high, but not as high as Virginia expected. But she was puzzled by the collateral clause. Collateral was not needed as long as the weekly payment was made on time. It was only if the couple defaulted on a payment that the loan shark would be free to take something from them. That something was left up to Vladimir to define if the need ever arose.

Jerry, not the best businessman, appeared not to notice anything strange about the terms. He agreed at once to Vladimir's terms. Noticing Virginia's frown, Vladimir favored her with another small smile. "The terms of this loan may never affect you, lovely lady," he purred as Jerry signed the papers. "It is your husband who has taken this loan and he who must pay the collateral, if it comes to that."

Jerry accepted the rent money from Vladimir, and the couple left the lovely apartment to descend the dingy stairs to the grocery below. Olga shook her head sadly when she saw Jerry pocketing the money on the way out. "Foolish boy. He will bleed you dry," she whispered.

The loan tided the couple over to the next paycheck, and things went better after that. Jerry tried to curb his antiques collecting, and Virginia saved every penny that wasn't needed for bills or Vladimir's loan payment. In this manner, she was able to buy a cheap dining-room table, two chairs, and a ratty old secondhand sofa for the living room.

Sometimes at night, Virginia dreamed about an elegant apartment with its cherry-red furnishings, velvet draperies, and lush sofas around a warm fireplace. The handsome man in these dreams was not her boyish husband. But she shrugged the nighttime fantasies aside to face the grim reality of life on a tight budget and a husband who still brought home unsuitable things, if not so often as before. *I truly love Jerry,* Virginia told herself each morning as she sat at the splintered table to drink the watered-down coffee that was all they could afford. She just wished he would grow up.

That evening Jerry thudded his way up to their apartment with a huge wagon wheel, which he nailed above the ratty old sofa. *Oh joy,* Virginia thought, staring at it glumly. *I wonder how much that cost?*

As it turned out, the wheel cost too much. The money Jerry used for the wagon wheel should have gone to Vladimir. "Don't worry about it," Jerry said to his angry wife. "I am sure Vladimir will understand."

Virginia, remembering the strange collateral clause, wasn't so sure. Olga's words came back to haunt her: "Vladimir will bleed you dry if you do not take care." *Oh, please let her be wrong,* she prayed frantically. They were already so poor. If Vladimir called in Jerry's loan, they would be out on the street. *At least you would be away from the wagon wheel,* a tiny voice whispered in the back of her mind. *And the stuffed elephant's foot and the spinning wheels and the old trombone . . .* For a moment, Virginia saw a candlelit room filled with cherry-red furnishings. She thrust the memory away.

Jerry bounded off, filled with confidence in his ability to persuade Vladimir to give them a break. He returned an hour later. He was pale and sweaty as he came through the door, almost feverish. It had obviously not been a good interview.

"Vladimir said I can give him both payments next week," he announced, falling onto the ratty sofa. Virginia sighed in relief. So he wasn't going to bleed them dry, as she had feared.

"Did he ask for collateral?" she inquired.

"Yes. But it was nothing major," Jerry said. His sharp tone forbade further questioning. Virginia was surprised and a little hurt by her husband's curt reply.

She went to the kitchen and heated up a can of soup for their supper. There were only three cans left between now and the next paycheck. She had to make them last. Taking in her husband's pale, drooping figure, she recklessly pulled out the last of the bread and made toast to go with the soup. Jerry obviously needed something to perk him up. Vladimir must have really raked him over the coals.

Jerry must have scraped together the money for the double payment the following week, because he didn't mention Vladimir again. Still, Virginia worried about her husband. Over the course of the next month, he aged dramatically. Streaks of gray appeared in his curly blond hair, and his face grew haggard and lined, as if he was in constant pain. Jerry's once-lively step became heavy and faltering. Once, he almost fainted in the bathroom while preparing for bed.

One evening as Virginia did laundry, she found blood on his shirt. Alarmed, she raced into the bedroom with the bloody shirt. Jerry laughed at her troubled face and told her he had cut himself shaving.

"I think you should see a doctor," Virginia told her husband. But he refused.

"I'm fine, honey," he said in the same sharp tone he'd used when she'd asked about the collateral. And that put an end to the conversation.

Two nights later, Jerry lurched in the door after work and collapsed against the huge hat rack, gasping with the effort of climbing the stairs. Hearing the thump, Virginia raced from the kitchen and stared aghast at her pale, shaking husband.

"Jerry," she screamed, running to catch him as he slid to the floor, giggling madly. There was no color in his face and neck, and even his hands seemed translucent.

"That devil really did bleed me dry," Jerry rasped, staring up into his frantic wife's face. With a shaking hand, he pulled aside his collar, and Virginia stared in horror at two puncture holes in the side of her husband's neck.

Suddenly, Jerry gasped, and his body arched in a brief spasm of pain. And just like that, Jerry was gone.

Dear God in heaven, Virginia thought, staring at her dead husband, who had been drained of every drop of blood he possessed. *Vladimir the loan shark is a vampire.*

In that moment of horror, a knock sounded on the front door. A plummy, sophisticated voice called through the door, "My dear Virginia, may I come in? We need to discuss the collateral on your loan."

18

Prison Break

Callahan was huddled in a cavern near the Pacific Ocean when the Feds closed in. There were still shreds of human flesh under his fingernails when the serial killer surrendered to the inevitable capture. The Feds could put him behind bars, he vowed as they dragged him down the narrow path toward the waiting cars, but he would escape. And then they'd be sorry. Callahan lashed out at the nearest officer, landing a crippling blow on his kneecap. The remaining men knocked him to the ground and bound his feet and hands to ensure his cooperation.

Callahan was sentenced to a lonely prison for the criminally insane, his only companions the wardens and fellow madmen. Over the next seventeen years, Callahan spent every spare second planning his escape. He studied every weakness in the prison system. He knew the movement of every guard. He spent several years contriving to get a ground-floor cell so he could dig his way out. That plan nearly succeeded, until he reached bedrock a few feet below the cell floor.

With every failed plan, Callahan's anger grew. He would escape this wretched cell if it killed him. And then he would track down the men who had captured him, kill them, and roast their bodies over an open fire—perhaps in the very cave in which he had been caught. Yes, that would be a fitting revenge.

As the years passed, Callahan noticed that one elderly prisoner, Old Ben, had become the general handyman and undertaker around the remote prison. It was Old Ben's job to put deceased prisoners into a pine coffin, where they lay overnight in the prison chapel. The next morning, Old Ben and the warden would ride out to the cemetery a mile or so outside the prison gates. Together, they would carry the coffin to the grave site and lower it within. Then the warden returned to the prison for his morning coffee, leaving Old Ben to bury the deceased.

Old Ben was the logical choice for such burial duty. He was far too old and rickety to try to escape into the wilderness. The warden could leave him to it, knowing that Old Ben would faithfully return to the prison when his job was finished.

Callahan could use an ally like Old Ben. Oh yes. Old Ben could sneak him out of the prison if anyone could. So Callahan befriended the handyman, listening to his long-winded rambling. He even helped the handyman with his chores. Once this "friendship" was firmly established, Callahan tried to gain the old man's sympathies. He spoke longingly of his desire to see his old home and visit his aging mother (who in truth was Callahan's first victim). He described his successful son (victim number two) and his lovely daughter (victim three), and how he had never seen his (nonexistent) grandchildren. Old Ben was swayed by the serial killer's heart-wrenching stories. When Callahan spoke of the plan he'd devised to win his freedom, Old Ben was ready to assist in any way he could.

Callahan's plan was simple. The next time a prisoner passed away, he would creep into the chapel after dark and slip into the coffin with the dead body. In the morning, the warden and Old Ben would take the coffin out of the prison to the cemetery to

125

PRISON BREAK

bury the deceased. As soon as the warden left, Old Ben would open the coffin and let Callahan out, with no one the wiser. It was a brilliant plan, and Old Ben agreed to help the murderer gain his freedom.

Unfortunately, the prisoners were very healthy that summer, and through the long, colorful autumn that followed. No one caught so much as a chill, and the new year came with no prisoner fatalities in more than eight months. It set a new prison record.

The warden was praised for this new record, and Callahan was infuriated by it. Day after day, he listened for the bell that tolled whenever a prisoner died, but it did not ring. Callahan was tempted to expedite matters by killing someone with his bare hands, but such an action—if discovered—would mean solitary confinement for the serial killer, and he would be unable to enact his brilliant plan. So he waited. And waited.

It was late February when the expected bell tolled dolefully through the prison. Snow was falling in the yard where Callahan marched with his fellow prisoners during their daily exercise routine when the bell rang. "I wonder who it is this time?" muttered a burly man just ahead of Callahan. The serial killer, hands shaking with joy, could care less who it was. The time had come! Tomorrow he would be free.

It was the longest afternoon Callahan had spent at the prison, waiting for the moment he was locked in for the night. Once the floor was clear of wardens, he broke out of his cell and moved like a shadow down the hall, hearing the snores of his fellow inmates for the last time.

Callahan entered the dark chapel and felt his way to the front. Yes, there was a coffin standing on top of two pine benches. He lifted the lid, and the smell of embalming chemicals filled his nostrils. He jerked back a little. Old Ben had done his job well. Callahan groped his way inside the coffin and lay down on top of the inert mass inside. Then he closed the lid.

As he lay in the coffin waiting for dawn, the serial killer felt his skin begin to crawl. He'd killed more than twenty-five people in his life without qualm or remorse, but this deathwatch made him itch all over. His heart pounded with fear of death, with fear of what came after death. What if there was nothing? What if there was something far worse than nothing? The chemical smell of the corpse below him made Callahan's stomach roil. Only the determination of seventeen years of planning kept him in the coffin. It would soon be over. In the morning he would be free of this foul air and of his rotting companion. Old Ben would free him as soon as the warden was gone. Old Ben would never let down his "friend."

Callahan must have dozed off toward dawn, in spite of his grisly companion. He was jolted awake in the complete darkness within the foul-smelling box when the coffin was lifted off the pine benches. He heard mumbled voices overhead. Old Ben and the warden must be moving the coffin to the waiting pony cart.

Callahan shivered as the cold February air encompassed the coffin. The temperature decreased dramatically, and he cursed himself for not remembering his coat. The cold would make it more difficult to escape into the wintery woods surrounding the prison. But if he stuck to the road, Callahan would find a house to break into before too long, even in this remote place.

The constant shaking of the coffin increased his nausea, but Callahan forced down the bile in his throat. *Almost free, almost free.* He chanted the words silently in his mind, ignoring the foul smell emanating from his dead companion.

Finally, the cart stopped and the coffin was lifted down. Callahan felt a thump as it landed in the bottom of the grave. His heart thudded with joy. Now was his moment. Now the warden would leave Old Ben to fill in the grave while he went back to the prison to have his morning coffee. Instead, something thudded onto the lid of the coffin just over Callahan's head. He strained his eyes against the pitch-darkness of the coffin. Was the warden saying last words over the body? Was he throwing a bit of symbolic dirt onto the coffin?

But the thudding continued unabated, and Callahan's heart pounded in sudden fear. They were burying the coffin with him in it! How could that be? Maybe the warden had stayed to help Old Ben? That was the answer. Old Ben was rather frail, and the warden was helping him. Old Ben would make some excuse and come back to free Callahan after the warden went in for his morning coffee.

The thudding grew fainter as the grave filled in above Callahan. After a few minutes, the foul air inside the coffin grew thin and hot, and the chemical smell was overwhelming. Callahan vomited all over his clothes before he could stop himself. When he rid himself of the contents of his stomach, Callahan pounded the lid of the coffin and shouted, "Come on, Old Ben! Kill the warden if you must! Hurry up, you . . ." Callahan cursed the old man in the foulest barracks language he knew and then coughed in the thin air, which reeked of embalming fluid and vomit.

Callahan took shallow breaths, trying to conserve his air. Panic roiled within his gut, and his whole body began to shake. The silence around him was the silence of the grave, stark and unbending and full of menace. Callahan frantically scratched at the lid above him until his fingernails split and drops of blood rained down on his face. He twisted and turned against the stiffening corpse, screaming, "Come on, Old Ben. Let me out, I beg you!" The final word ended in a panicked sob. The answering silence was deafening. Callahan's ears rang with it. He swallowed down more bile. The air in the coffin was stifling hot, and he was growing dizzy from lack of oxygen. He could hardly think straight. The smell of embalming fluid and rot filled his nostrils and filled his brain, filled his whole world . . .

A horrifying thought struck Callahan, bringing him back to full consciousness in a moment of tingling terror that tightened every muscle in his body. What if Old Ben was not coming to rescue him? What if . . . ?

Callahan fumbled in his pocket and removed a match with trembling hands. It took Callahan three tries to light it. In the sudden flickering brightness, the serial killer turned his head and looked over his shoulder into the pale dead face of Old Ben.

19

Bloody Mary's Mirror

I was antiques shopping in Lancaster, Pennsylvania, when I saw a small hand mirror tucked away on a back shelf of a creaky old barn. It was blackened with age, about nine inches long and four wide with an applied cast and chased border. Probably eighteenth-century Dutch, my collector's eye gauged. The mirror, which was shaped like an elongated three-leaf clover, was obviously the lone survivor of a lady's fine toilette set. I picked the mirror up and discovered it was heavier than it appeared. I realized that the mirror was solid silver underneath the tarnish. What a find!

I carried the mirror to the front of the barn, where a plump middle-aged woman in a cap and long skirt sat minding the register. When I placed the hand mirror on the counter, the woman's eyes widened. "Fancy you finding that old thing," she said to me. "It's been handed down in my brother-in-law's family for more generations than I care to count." She named a price far lower than I estimated the mirror would be worth once it was cleaned up, so I handed her my credit card.

As she rang up the charge, the woman reminisced, "They call it the Gansmueller mirror. There's an old family legend attached to the mirror. It's just a lot of fairy-tale nonsense, to my mind. But I know you antiques collectors love a good story."

"What is the story?" I asked eagerly.

The woman measured out some tape and secured the tissue paper around the mirror. Then she said, "The mirror once belonged to a woman named Mary Gansmueller, who was burned as a witch in the late 1700s." She watched me expectantly.

I frowned. A witch named Mary Gansmueller. It rang a faint bell in my mind, but the knowledge eluded me.

The plump farmwife gave me another hint. "Frau Gansmueller is said to have used this mirror in her black-magic spells. It was one of three mirrors she had in her possession. Two were smashed by the angry mob that burned her at the stake. This third mirror was found at the bottom of an old herb basket that Frau Gansmueller used to carry around the village. One morning, she left the basket with my brother-in-law's many times great-grandmother, who was her cousin. She asked her cousin to watch over its contents should anything happen to her. Frau Gansmueller had some presentiment that she was going to die."

"How horrible for her," I said with a shiver.

"Not really," the woman replied. "Frau Gansmueller was just as evil as the villagers claimed. She murdered several young children and used their blood to make herself young again. With her dying breath, she is said to have laid a terrible curse on every mirror that was ever made."

That's when I realized who Frau Gansmueller was. My eyes nearly popped out of their sockets. "You are saying this mirror was once owned by Bloody Mary?"

"We don't use that name in our house," the woman said primly, pursing her lips in disapproval.

I apologized and begged her to continue the story.

"That's it, really," she said, putting the wrapped mirror into a shopping bag and handing it to me. "My brother-in-law didn't tell me the whole story. He knows I don't hold with hocus-pocus."

I felt rather let down by this feeble ending to such a dramatic tale. Still, I thanked the woman and carried the mirror to my car, marveling at my lucky find.

I spent the whole day exploring antiques shops and then had a late supper at a wonderful Pennsylvania Dutch restaurant, where I gorged myself on shoofly pie. Feeling a bit bloated, I drove home and wrestled my many packages through my front door.

"Good lord," said my husband, coming out of his study to help me with my purchases. "I think you bought every antique in the county!"

"Pretty close," I said.

One by one, I uncovered my treasures and showed them to my patient spouse. Thomas had no interest in anything older than last week. Still, his eyes lit up when I pulled the antique hand mirror out of the shopping bag and unwrapped the tissue paper.

"I think it's solid silver," I told him. "And it has this crazy story attached to it." I told him about Frau Gansmueller and the curse.

"So you bought Bloody Mary's mirror?" he asked with a grin. "How brave of you."

Taking it from my hand, he studied the mirror from every angle. "I've got some silver polish in my study. I can shine it up real nice." He vanished into his study with the mirror

BLOODY MARY'S MIRROR

and left me blissfully unpacking the rest of my treasures in the living room.

Twenty minutes later, I heard Thomas shriek from inside his study. My husband never raised his voice for anything less than an emergency, so I raced into the room, expecting anything from a broken arm to a fire. I found Thomas leaning heavily against his desk and the half-polished hand mirror on the floor, its unbroken glass brilliantly reflecting the overhead light.

"What's wrong? Are you ill?" I gasped, clutching his shoulder in concern. I could feel Thomas shaking under my hand.

"Th . . . that thing," Thomas gasped, gesturing down at the mirror. "For a moment, I thought someone was . . . was *looking* at me out of the mirror." He shuddered all over and turned his back on the glittering object at our feet.

I stared at the hand mirror and then at my levelheaded, unimaginative husband. What in the world? Tiny hairs prickled all along my arms, and the flesh just above my elbows grew cold.

The smell of silver polish wafting through the air broke the spell. My nose twitched at the scent and I sneezed. The mood in the room shifted from fear to farce, and Thomas gave a shaky laugh. "I'm sure it was all my imagination. Darn that woman for telling you such a silly tale!" He handed me his pocket handkerchief, and I wiped my nose with a grin.

"I'll finish polishing it in a jiffy," he said in a normal tone. He grabbed polish, cloths, and the mirror and followed me back into the living room. "I want to see the rest of your purchases," he said amiably, settling down into his rocking chair by the fireplace. I glanced at him sharply. His tone was normal, but his hands still shook as he took up the mirror and started polishing another tarnished section. Obviously, the incident with the mirror had shaken my husband more than he was willing to admit. Thomas had zero interest in antiques.

The clover-shaped hand mirror was absolutely lovely once it was polished. It sparkled in the firelight, and you could see all the lovely flowers and ornamentation framing the sides and pistol-shaped handle.

"We should hang it on the living-room wall by the door," I suggested. "You could make a bracket for it."

Thomas, who loved to carve, agreed at once. He pulled out paper and pencil and started sketching a small hanging bracket ornamented with three-leaf clovers and flowers to complement the mirror. His unexpected fright in the study was completely forgotten.

I paused often over the next few days to admire my new purchase hanging in its lovely carved bracket on the living-room wall. Whenever I gazed into the hand mirror, I felt younger and much prettier than anyone (except Thomas) imagined me to be. My wrinkles seemed to vanish in its silvery depths, and time moved backward by several decades. Instead of an empty nester, I was a young bride again, just moving into my first house with my handsome husband.

In other ways, things weren't going particularly well in our house. The bathroom and bedroom mirrors were behaving strangely. Whenever I looked into them, I saw shapes moving at the edge of my vision. But when I turned my head, nothing was there. Sometimes when I was alone in the house, I heard a humming sound, and the air seemed to shimmer inside the living room. It was creepy.

The first time this happened, our cat rose up spitting from his accustomed place on the back of the couch and ran outside through the cat door in the kitchen. He refused to come back inside. Thomas had to leave cat food out on the back patio so he wouldn't starve.

About a week after I brought home the mirror, I was walking down the hall to the master bedroom when I saw a flat black shadow outlined against the wall to my right. It was the silhouette of a tall angular woman with one hand outstretched toward me. I screamed, pressing myself against the opposite wall and flinging up my hands to ward off the black figure. Thomas burst out of his study with an answering shout, and the shadow vanished immediately. I burst into tears, and Thomas swept me into his arms as I tried incoherently to explain the unexplainable.

The next morning I heard Thomas curse in the bathroom of our master suite, and the electric razor abruptly turned off. I hurried over to see what was wrong and found him dabbing at a scratch down his left cheek.

"Darn razor cut me," he said, holding toilet paper against his cheek to stop the bleeding.

"But it's a safety razor," I said, staring in shock at my bleeding husband. "How could it cut you?"

When Thomas removed the toilet paper, I saw two bloody vertical lines running from cheekbone to chin. It looked as if something had clawed him.

I glanced into the brightly lit mirror. For a moment, I thought I saw a pair of black eyes glaring back at me. I gasped, and Thomas quickly looked up from his bloody tissue. But the mirror was empty.

Dear God, I must be going crazy, I thought, knees weak with shock. I mumbled something about fetching the first-aid kit and ran out of the bathroom. As I passed the dressing table, I glanced into the mirror and saw a black shadow figure encased in flames looming behind me. I whirled with a shriek of terror. There was nothing between me and the bed, but I could feel an invisible menace shimmering in the air in front. The sensation pulsed along my skin, sending icy chills through my blood and raising goose bumps all over my body. "Go away!" I screamed. "Go away!"

Thomas leapt from the bathroom, his cheek still bleeding freely. But I was already fleeing down the hallway, trying to get away from the black menace. One thought dominated my terrified mind: I had to get that horrible antique hand mirror out of my house right now, before Bloody Mary killed us both.

All around me, I could hear someone laughing. It was a high-pitched evil cackle with the crackle of flames behind it. I rounded the corner and burst into the living room. The clover-shaped mirror was directly in front of me. It looked as large as a building to my nerve-frazzled eyes, as if it covered the whole world. I saw a lovely face in the mirror. It was my face, looking just as it had the day I was married.

My fear faded into a dazed euphoria. I walked toward the mirror, my eyes fixed on the lovely face within. If I stepped inside, I would be that woman again—ageless, forever young. My lips parted with delight as I stepped in front of the mirror.

And then the face became that of a dark-haired woman with a twisted visage and wicked black eyes. I reeled backward in shock just as Bloody Mary reached out of the mirror with clawed hands and grabbed my cheeks. I felt her nails bite into me as she dragged me toward her. The mirror burst into flames, and I felt my hair burning, my skin blackening. The whole world spun around me in an agony of pain.

"Mine! You are mine," a woman's evil voice hissed in my ears.

Suddenly, a pair of strong arms clamped around my middle and pulled me backward out of the mirror. The woman within screamed and lashed out, her sharp nails scraping all the way down to my chin before they released me.

Thomas carried me, sobbing and bleeding profusely, through the front door. "We are leaving right now," he said grimly, cradling me against him as I bled all over his shirt. I could smell smoke in our clothes, and half my hair had been burnt away.

From somewhere over my shoulder, a man's voice called, "It looks like you folks could use a hand."

I wiped blood from my throbbing cheeks and raised my head to look for the source of the voice. A jolly-faced, dark-eyed stranger wearing overalls and a farmer's straw hat stood beside a truck that was parked in front of our house.

Thomas's arms tightened around me. "Not sure there's anything you can do for us, mister, but thanks for asking."

"I'm not so sure about that," said the stranger, shrewdly eyeing the blood dripping down both our faces. "My name's Gansmueller. My sister-in-law sold you an antique mirror about a week ago."

I gasped and then gestured for Thomas to put me down.

"She wasn't supposed to sell the mirror," the farmer continued. "One of my kids swiped it from the old chest a couple of months ago and used it to frighten his sister. The kids dropped it in the antiques barn and couldn't find it when I sent them to retrieve it. We reckon a shopper must have found it and put it on that shelf. When you brought it to the register, my sister-in-law thought we'd finally come to our senses and decided to sell the cursed thing."

Mr. Gansmueller handed me his bandana to press against my bloody cheeks. "We tracked down your name and address from your credit card receipt, and I came to ask if you would sell it back to us," he said. "To tell the truth, I really wanted to check to make sure you are all right. There's a curse on that mirror, and you have to handle it properly to keep the dark spirit contained. It should never have gone out of the family."

"We are not all r . . . right," I said, my voice shaken all to pieces. "I want that mirror out of my house right now. Can you do that?"

"Ma'am, I can. And I will put your money back on your credit card right away," Mr. Gansmueller added. "Where is the hand mirror now?"

Thomas described its location and then helped me over to a garden bench by the flowerbed. We sat huddled together as Mr. Gansmueller vanished into our cursed house. A moment later, we heard a thump. A silent scream blew our hair away from our faces in a mighty draft of evil anger. The whole house shook. For a moment, we smelled smoke and brimstone, and the windows in the living room flashed so bright that we had to close our eyes against the glare. Then silence returned.

I was still seeing bright spots when Mr. Gansmueller emerged from the house with the silver hand mirror in hand. He was a mess, hair disheveled and clothes black with soot. There were scratches on his bare forearms and one on his chin. Thomas rose to his feet in alarm and called to him. Gansmueller limped over to the garden bench and said, "I'm afraid the living room is an unholy mess. But the spirit is back in the mirror. It's safe to go inside."

"Are you all right?" I asked, staring in alarm from his white face to the glowing mirror clutched in his hand.

"I'll be fine, ma'am," Gansmueller said. "Once I get this mirror back home where it belongs."

"Thank you for rescuing us," Thomas said, pulling me to my feet and hugging me close.

We watched as Mr. Gansmueller got into his truck and drove away with Bloody Mary's mirror.

"I think we should stop by Saint Catherine's and ask Father Schubert to come pray over our house before we go back inside," Thomas said.

"I think that's a very good idea," I said.

Our cat appeared for the first time in days, oozing out from under a hydrangea bush and rubbing against my leg. I took this as a hopeful sign. I picked him up, and the three of us got in our car and drove straight to the church to talk to Father Schubert.

20

The Bloody Handkerchief

He killed my daughter. The master just murdered my only child.
The words rang through Jack's mind as the voodoo man knelt
on the floor beside Jo's body. His daughter lay like a battered
rag doll at the foot of the drinks cabinet in a pool of her own
blood. Jack dragged his shocked gaze from Jo and looked at the
occupants of the fancy dining-room table. The master sat at one
end, his wife at the other. A son and daughter sat on either side.
Wife, son, and daughter stared aghast at the serving girl lying
on the floor, blood still dripping from a huge dent in her right
temple. At the head of the table, the master glared irritably at
the dying girl and snapped, "Take the useless baggage out of
here! She spilled gravy all over the tablecloth."

Jack gazed in disbelief at the small gravy stain by the master's
plate. All of this anger, this unthinking violence, because of a
tiny spill? Beside him, Jo's lips parted. She gave a soft moan and
then died, right there on the floor. "And clean up that blood,"
the master shouted at Jack, waving the heavy ladle he'd used to
bash in the side of Jo's head.

Jack's lips thinned with anger. The voodoo man wanted to
leap to his feet and attack the murdering master right there and
then. Then his eyes fell on the pungent puddle of Jo's warm

142

blood, and a thought struck him. Why should he give the master a quick death? That would be too easy.

Jack pulled out his white handkerchief and carefully wiped up every drop of his beloved daughter's blood. Then he carefully carried her out of the dining room and took her to her stunned mother to prepare for burial. Back in the plantation house, he could hear the master shouting for the butler to bring more gravy and berating his poor wife for not eating. Jack fingered the bloody handkerchief in his pocket and smiled.

In his tiny slave cabin, he watched his wife tenderly wash and dress their dead daughter's corpse while he assembled the objects needed for a voodoo spell of vengeance. On the table he placed black candles, a cow's brain, and nine cayenne peppers. Finally, he put the white handkerchief, still damp with his precious daughter's blood, beside the rest and prepared himself mentally and physically for the ritual ahead.

A week after the murder, Jack stole into the front yard at dusk and dropped a piece of the bloody handkerchief in front of a plantation cat. The frisky feline pounced on the handkerchief and batted it this way and that across the lawn. Inside the house, the master's wife giggled suddenly and started batting at the air with her hands. She leapt from her chair and pounced on an invisible spot on the floor. Outside in the yard, the wind grabbed the handkerchief and blew it up and down and all around. Inside the house, the wife whirled around and around, chasing something invisible up and down the length of the parlor while her goggle-eyed children watched in amazement. They could hear her purring.

Hearing the commotion, the master strode into the room and frowned at his wife's antics. "Stop that, Matilda!" he

THE BLOODY HANDKERCHIEF

shouted. His wife whirled and hissed. Then she lashed out at him, fingers extended like claws. Her nails raked down his cheeks, leaving bloody scratches behind. She hunched her back and ran from the room with a yowl. Out in the yard, the cat yowled in sympathy and ran for the barn. Her searching husband found wife and cat crouched together in the hayloft. Neither would come down until he left the barn.

During the course of the next month, the master's wife grew more feral with each passing day. She purred and rubbed lovingly against her children but fiercely attacked her husband whenever he drew near. In despair, the master had his wife placed in an asylum.

Jack watched from the door of his slave cabin as a closed carriage carried his former mistress down the oak-lined driveway and out of sight. Then he went to the special carved box where he kept objects used in his voodoo religion and removed a second piece of the bloody handkerchief. At dusk, he went to the stable and buried the handkerchief in the straw under the hoof of an ornery brute of a mule that the master kept for pulling his carts. The mule lifted its foot to kick the voodoo man, thought better of it, and put back its ears instead.

At the master's dining-room table, the son threw back his head and brayed. The master's head whipped around. "Theodore, stop that!" he shouted. The son knocked over his chair and trotted out of the room on all fours as the master and his daughter stared wide-eyed after the boy. The master threw down his napkin and raced after his son. He was kicked in the stomach as soon as he exited the door. He tumbled backward onto his backside, and his son kicked him again in the privates.

The master gasped and curled up in sudden agony. His son kicked him a third time in the back and trotted outside.

When he had recovered enough to limp after his son, the master found the boy in the stall with the ornery mule, calmly eating hay. The son kicked the master in the left leg when he approached the stall, and the mule kicked him in the right. The master was forced to leave his son in the barn.

The daughter was the only one who could approach the boy. She had to put a halter and lead line on him before he would leave the barn. When the son stopped next to the cart and tried to step between the traces, the master covered his face with his hands in despair. Two weeks later, the son was loaded into the asylum's closed carriage, kicking and braying madly as he strained against his lead line. Jack watched his antics from the door of his cabin.

At dusk, the voodoo man climbed a tree beside the house and dropped a piece of bloody handkerchief into a raven's nest. A moment later, the raven returned to the tree, cawing in indignation when it found an invader in its home. Ten minutes after that, the third-floor window opened and the daughter of the house climbed up onto the roof. Perched on a gable, she stuck her head under her arm and fell asleep.

At dawn the next morning, the master was awakened by a soprano cawing outside his bedroom window. It did not sound like the gravel-toned caw of a crow; it sounded like the voice of a young girl pretending to be a crow. The panicked master threw off his covers and raced outside. On the gabled roof, his daughter flapped her arms and cawed to the sunrise, shaking her flaxen curls to preen them in the light of the new day. Beside her, a large raven ruffled its feathers and blinked lazily down at the master.

"Serena, come down," the master begged in a defeated tone, his face gray with pain. Then he realized the foolishness of this request. "No, Serena, I take that back. Stay right there! Do *not* try to fly!"

The master ran toward the barn to fetch a ladder. Behind him, the raven launched itself into the air, cawing joyfully. Serena cawed, too, and flapped her arms. The master whirled in panic when he heard the raven's caw and hurtled back toward the house. Before his eyes, Serena fell in slow motion toward the hard, hard ground.

It was dusk a few days later when the townsfolk gathered in the family cemetery at the back of the plantation. The minister spoke solemn words over the newest grave and threw a few clumps of soil onto the coffin. One by one the mourners followed suit. The master stood weeping beside the new headstone as his slaves filled in the grave. Within the space of two months, he had lost his entire family.

The funeral party departed in ones and twos, leaving the master alone with his grief. As the master knelt beside the newly filled grave, a sympathetic hand pressed against his shoulder. He glanced up into the voodoo man's dark eyes.

"I know what it's like to lose a daughter," Jack said and walked solemnly away. Behind him, the master frowned at the audacity of this negative reminder and impatiently brushed a piece of bloody handkerchief from the shoulder of his coat.

At the edge of the woods, a large black wolf lifted its muzzle and sniffed the air. It smelled blood. The wolf howled once to alert his pack and then trotted into the cemetery. Beside the grave, the master threw back his head and howled back.

21

Mothman

They were too excited to go straight home after the prom, so the group headed to the local Soda Shoppe to drink root beer floats and flirt with their dates. Natalie was thrilled to be out late on this special night, in spite of the dreary rain that threatened to frizz her hair. Her prom date, Alex, was captain of the football team and considered the best catch in school. Natalie had won a lot of popularity points when he'd asked her to be his date at the prom.

When the root beer floats arrived, Tim—who was dating Natalie's friend Annie—leaned forward and waggled his eyebrows at the two girls. "I hear the Mothman has been seen just outside town," he said in a frightening voice, "waiting to pounce on pretty girls and eat their hearts out."

"Ha, ha. Very funny," Annie said with a frown.

Natalie frowned in confusion. "Who is the Mothman?" she asked. Natalie had moved to town at the beginning of the school year and still didn't know all the local legends.

Tim and Alex were happy to fill her in on the Mothman. As they sipped their sodas, the boys told Natalie the following legend.

There was once a scientist who worked on top-secret government projects at a local chemical plant during World War II. The scientist was developing a chemical weapon from the poison of South American moths that would destroy the enemy and bring a rapid end to the war. He worked long hours, late into the night, and grew so tired that he started making mistakes. One night the beaker where he brewed his deadly concoctions exploded right in his face. The scientist was blown through the wall of his office and lay on the floor of the hallway, writhing in desperate pain as chemicals burned through his body. As the top-secret potion mixed with the scientist's body chemicals, the man started mutating. Great mothlike wings burst from his shoulder blades; his arms and legs elongated; claws formed on his fingers and toes; and his eyes glowed red with fire. His incisors became fangs that bit right through his lips, tearing them to shreds. The mutated scientist licked hungrily at the blood with his striped tongue, and the taste awakened another fire in his gut—a deep, burning desire for human flesh.

The accident in the lab had triggered the alarm bell. Night watchmen ran into the hallway and came face-to-face with the new monster. They were the first to die. One man escaped into a guard booth and called in another alarm while the monster tore at the door with superhuman strength. The guard's frantic babbling was cut off by a sudden scream as the monster tore out his heart with its sharp claws. His dying words were: "Mothman. Save us from the Mothman." The phone dropped from his lifeless hand as the newly christened Mothman sank down on its haunches and devoured the man's dripping heart, chuckling in delight as blood spattered its twisted face. By the time the police arrived, the monster had vanished into the mountainous forest behind the chemical factory

"The Mothman is still out there, waiting for unsuspecting people to walk in the woods so he can eat their hearts," Tim concluded gleefully.

Natalie shuddered. She couldn't help it. Alex laughed and threw his arm over her shoulders. "Why don't I drive Natalie home so she feels safe," he said. "You and Annie can wait for the bill, right, Tim?"

Alex tossed his buddy some cash and hustled Natalie out of the Soda Shoppe with a broad wink. Natalie heard Annie giggling. They both knew why Tim and Alex had told such a scary story. The boys thought the girls would be ready to do some snuggling after receiving such a scare. And Natalie had to admit, the idea of cuddling with Alex was very appealing. He was really cute!

Natalie wasn't surprised when Alex pulled off onto a remote country road about halfway home and proposed parking for a while. She blushed demurely and agreed. Just as Alex slipped his arm around her, the car shook from front to back, as if struck by a mighty wind. Natalie gave a small shriek and clutched his shirt in alarm. "What was that?" she cried. "Was it the Mothman?"

Alex laughed. "Relax, darling. It's just a thunderstorm." He pulled her close.

"I'm scared," Natalie said. She thought she had seen a dark shadow pass over the car just after the wind shook it. In her mind, she pictured a twisted face with fangs eating the security guard's bleeding heart.

"Relax, babe," Alex said and kissed her. Alex was a good kisser. Natalie forgot her fear and kissed him back.

Suddenly, the whole vehicle rocked on its wheels as something large landed on the roof with a huge thump. Natalie pulled away from Alex with a shriek.

"What was that?"

"The wind just knocked a branch onto the roof," Alex said, trying to kiss her again.

"I want to go home," Natalie said, her voice trembling with fear.

A high-pitched whine came from the roof. It sounded like claws were scraping the metal. Natalie screamed. "The Mothman is here! Alex, I want to go home."

"It's just the tree branch scratching the top of the car," Alex said. "Come on, Natalie. We never have time to ourselves. Just ignore it."

But Natalie was too scared to stay. "Take me home, Alex," she repeated stubbornly.

"Look, if it makes you happy, I will pull the branch off the car," Alex said, hopping out into the rain before Natalie could protest. He stuck his head back in the door and said, "Lock the door behind me if it makes you feel better. I'll knock when I've got the branch off the car."

Natalie locked the door behind Alex and sat listening to the rain thudding against the car as Alex disappeared into the darkness. She heard a sudden thump overhead, and the car rocked a third time. That must have been Alex pulling the branch off the roof. The car rocked once more, and a puff of wind rattled the windows. Then everything grew still save the gentle patter of the rain. One minute passed and then two. Natalie shivered and rubbed the goose bumps on her arms as she waited for Alex to knock on the door. She swallowed nervously when he did not appear. *He is probably going to jump at my window and make me scream,* she told herself. Alex could be so juvenile sometimes.

But Alex still did not appear.

Natalie was steeling herself to get out of the car to look for her boyfriend when she saw flashing red and blue lights approaching along the road. Relief flooded her, making her

MOTHMAN

light-headed. Thank God, the police had come. She and Alex would probably get in trouble for parking, but Natalie didn't care. She just wanted to find Alex and go home.

Suddenly, the police car slammed on its brakes and two men leapt out. Then Alex's car shook as a thunderous wind rushed around it. Something scraped the roof over Natalie's head, and she could hear the police officers firing their guns. Natalie screamed as a huge dark shadow flew off into the night.

One of the officers ran to Alex's car and pounded on her door. Still screaming, Natalie unlocked it and threw herself into his arms. The officer hustled her toward the police car as something unearthly screamed above them. Natalie ducked instinctively as the horrible flapping creature dive-bombed them. The police officer pushed Natalie to the ground and shielded her with his body. The monster's claws ripped his back to shreds right through his bulletproof vest. Natalie heard the second officer fire two more shots. Then she heard the monster fly away over the trees.

Tears and mud coursed down Natalie's face as the wounded officer pulled her up and helped her into the patrol car. "My date," she cried suddenly. "Alex was outside with that . . . that thing! What happened to Alex?"

The officers looked grave and shook their heads. "Don't look, miss," the first officer said. But Natalie couldn't help herself. She glanced at the parked vehicle, illuminated by the flashing lights of the patrol car, and saw massive claw marks etched into the hood. A small bundle huddled on top of the rain-soaked roof. For a moment, Natalie's eyes refused to understand what they were seeing. Then the officer touched the bundle, and Alex's head fell toward the headlights, blue eyes staring blankly at nothing, face twisted in a rictus of fear. His chest was gaping open, and his half-chewed heart lay on the muddy ground at the officer's feet.

22

The Clown Mannequin

Jan arrived promptly at 6:45 p.m. for her babysitting job. The Smiths lived in a rambling old farmhouse set in the middle of a fenced-in yard. Rhododendrons lined one side of the house and Rose of Sharon bushes dominated the other. In front was an overgrown English garden, and in back was a large lawn perfect for football games. Jan loved the Smiths' house. She hoped to own a place like this someday, when she was a rich and famous author. But for now, Jan appreciated the chance to hang out in such a lovely house with two rambunctious but enjoyable twin boys.

Normally, the boys and their Yorkshire terrier, Lady, came spilling out the front door when Jan arrived. Tonight, Jan found herself walking to the front door of the old house unaccompanied. This was highly suspicious. Mrs. Smith opened the front door with a smile and greeting. A moment later, two syrupy-sweet voices called to Jan from upstairs, "Jan! Come up and look at our comic book collection." This was extremely suspicious behavior. Mrs. Smith gave her a meaningful grimace that confirmed Jan's theory: The Smith boys were up to something.

Jan carefully climbed the stairs and walked down the hall, expecting the boys to jump out at her any second. Nothing happened. She knocked on the twins' bedroom door. "Come in," the boys called. Jan swung the door open warily and found herself facing a menacing six-foot-tall clown mannequin. It leered evilly at her through white-lashed red eyes, its large red grin painted so wide it nearly touched the too-large ears. A happy spotted hat bagged over one ear and matched the ludicrous red-spotted baggy pants, which were held up by red suspenders over a white shirt.

Jan shrieked in horror and stumbled backward out of the room. She tripped on the edge of the hall rug and sat down hard. Inside the bedroom, the twins laughed hysterically and their little Yorkie barked. The dog ran into the hall to frisk around the humiliated Jan as the twins rolled on the floor at the mannequin's feet.

"I told you she'd be frightened," cried Eddie.

"Say hi to our new friend," leered Freddie, grabbing the mannequin's shirt and walking it toward Jan.

"That thing is hideous," Jan said, pulling herself upright on the hall table. Her legs were shaking so badly she could hardly walk. "Why do you have such a hideous thing in your room? Clowns are creepy!"

"Hahaha," chortled Freddie. "Clowns are creepy!" He thrust the mannequin's hand toward Jan. "How do you do?" he asked in a fake deep voice.

"Ugh," Jan said, avoiding the mannequin's hand. Close up, she could see the elastic band that attached the clown mask to the mannequin's head. "I don't know how you can stand to keep such a creepy thing in your room! I will be downstairs if you twin nightmares need me!"

Jan stalked out of the room and slammed the door behind her. That mannequin was truly horrible. There was something so eerie about a clown. You could never tell what they were thinking behind the makeup. Ugh!

Downstairs, Mrs. Smith was looking for her glasses and Mr. Smith was adjusting his tie, using the stainless-steel refrigerator as a looking glass.

"You have our cell-phone number?" Mrs. Smith said. "And the number of the police station? And you know to call 9-1-1 if there is a fire or some emergency?"

Jan grinned. Mrs. Smith always ran through this litany before going out. Jan solemnly assured her that she knew what to do in an emergency.

"The Dantes are home tonight," Mrs. Smith continued, gesturing to the blue ranch house next door. "You can always run over there for help if there's a fire."

"There won't be a fire," Mr. Smith said, smoothing down his rather crooked tie. "Don't worry, Martha."

"I've heard there's an escaped convict on the loose in the next county," Mrs. Smith continued, ignoring her husband. "That serial killer who killed all those children in Virginia. So be sure to lock the doors behind us."

"Martha, you are going to scare Jan so bad she won't babysit for us again," Mr. Smith complained. "Come on. We are going to be late for our dinner reservations."

Mrs. Smith called the twins downstairs to kiss them good-bye and asked them to set the table for Jan. As she breezed out the back door, she called, "Dinner is in the oven. And remember to lock up behind us."

Jan hurried around the house, locking all the doors. Between the creepy clown mannequin upstairs and Mrs. Smith's talk of an escaped serial killer, she wasn't taking any chances.

Once she was done locking up, she pulled a casserole out of the oven, and everyone sat down at the table to eat dinner. Lady begged winsomely beside the twins' chairs until they caved in and gave her a bite from their plates. The Yorkie was trotting purposefully toward Jan when her head went up and she stopped to listen. A moment later, she bounded out of the kitchen and ran upstairs. Jan heard her barking at something in the twins' room. Then she heard a thud and the barking stopped abruptly. "What was that? Is something wrong?" she asked the twins.

"Nah," said Freddie. "Lady likes to bark at the squirrels in the oak tree outside our window."

"She jumps on the bed and throws herself at the glass," Eddie added, spooning more casserole onto his plate. "Sometimes she knocks her head so hard she gets dizzy and has to lie down. Silly dog."

The little Yorkie was still upstairs when the twins and Jan finished dinner. "I'm pretty full. How about we wait for a few minutes to eat our ice cream?" Jan suggested.

The twins clutched their full stomachs and agreed.

"Let's run upstairs and check on Lady," Jan said. "Then we can watch your favorite TV show. It starts at eight."

The twins cheered at both these suggestions. They charged upstairs and burst into their room, calling for Lady. Jan, jogging at their heels, reeled back a step or two when she saw the clown mannequin by the window. It was almost as much of a shock on the second viewing as it had been on the first.

Jan frowned suddenly. Something was different in here. Hadn't the clown mannequin been standing in the center of the room? The boys must have moved it after playing their practical joke on her.

On the far side of the room, the twins were kneeling on the floor, looking under the bunk beds for Lady.

THE CLOWN MANNEQUIN

"She's not in here. She must be downstairs in her basket," Eddie said. "Come on." He rushed away and Freddie followed. Jan cast one last shuddering glance at the clown mannequin before following the boys. For a moment, she thought she saw its chest move. And was that a blink? *Ridiculous,* she said to herself, goose bumps all over her body. *I hate clowns.* She hurried down the stairs, glad to get away from the creepy mannequin.

"Lady is in her basket in the laundry room," Freddie announced as Jan hurried into the front hall. "She's sleeping. She must have knocked her head really hard against the window."

Jan peeked in at Lady, who was curled up on the splotchy white cushion in her basket. There were wet paw prints leading toward the basket. Jan wondered if the washing machine was leaking. Before she could investigate, Eddie called to her from the living room, and she hurried to answer him. She'd check on Lady once the twins had settled down to watch their show.

In the kitchen, Jan scooped vanilla ice cream into two bowls. Then she went into the living room and handed the bowls to the twins, who were already absorbed in their cartoon. Freddie looked up suddenly and said, "Jan, I forgot to bring my bike in from the yard, and it's supposed to rain tonight. Would you please get it for me?"

Jan gave the tousle-haired boy a mock frown. "After the scare you gave me with that clown, I should make you do it!"

Freddie clasped his hands in supplication and gave her a cherubic grin. Jan relented. "All right, you monster. Watch your show. I'll be right back, so don't eat all the ice cream!"

Jan jogged out through the back door and glanced around the yard. No bike. Freddie must have left it on the side of the house. She circled the premises clockwise until she saw Freddie's bike lying between the oak tree and the rhododendrons. As she picked up the bike, she glimpsed a funny-shaped clump lying in the bushes under the twins' window. Jan wheeled the bike over to take a look.

Something about the huddled shape made Jan's skin feel clammy and her knees shake. It resembled a human body. But that was nonsense! Jan had to force herself to take a closer look. To her horror, Jan saw a naked mannequin lying under the bushes, stripped of its gaudy clothing and clown mask. Chills ran through Jan's body at the sight. Dear God. If the mannequin was down here, than what—or *who*—was upstairs in the boys' bedroom?

Panicked, Jan dropped Freddie's bike and sprinted frantically for the back door and the TV-watching twins. The vision of the too-still form of Lady lying in the basket replayed itself in her mind. She'd wondered about the funny splotches on the white cushion. They'd looked like splotches of blood. And wet paw prints on the floor leading to the basket. *Dear God, don't let me be too late!*

Jan spun around the corner into the living room and stopped in heartfelt relief. The boys were still sitting on the couch, absorbed in their cartoon. They looked up in surprise at her sudden entrance. Putting her finger to her lips, Jan beckoned mysteriously to them, hoping their curiosity would overcome their desire to watch TV. Eddie and Freddie glanced questioningly at her. They opened their mouths to speak, but she shook her head and beckoned again. Silently, the boys came over to Jan, who caught each of them by an arm and hustled them out the back door and over to the neighbor's house without explanation. Once the twins were safe with the Dantes,

Jan dialed 9-1-1 and begged the police to send someone over to check the house. Then she called the Smiths and told them to come home at once.

"I am probably being silly," she said to Mrs. Dante. "But I'm sure it was the twins' mannequin lying in the bushes, yet I saw the clown mannequin upstairs!"

An unmarked police car pulled into the driveway, and Jan ran to meet it so she could explain what she'd seen in the twins' room. The police officers sent her back to the Dantes' home to wait while they checked the house. The Smiths arrived, and Jan was trying to explain to the frantic parents the reason she'd called the police when gunshots exploded upstairs. Jan screamed as a man in a clown costume plunged backward through the twin's bedroom window, glass shattering everywhere. The man hit the ground with a loud thud and lay still at the base of the rhododendrons as more police officers drove up to the house. In the flashing red and blue lights cast by the police cars, Jan could see that the dead clown had landed right beside the body of the mannequin that he had replaced in the bedroom.

Much later, the police told Jan and the Smith family that the escaped serial killer had climbed the oak tree, crept into the twins' bedroom, and disguised himself as a clown, throwing the incriminating mannequin into the bushes where it wouldn't be seen. He had slit the little Yorkie's throat when she barked at him, and the poor mite had crept downstairs to bleed to death in her basket while the killer waited upstairs for the twins' bedtime. If Jan had not seen the mannequin when she went outside to pick up Freddie's bike, the boys and Jan would have been murdered.

23

Assassin

Jean-Claude was tying his cravat in front of the full-length mirror in his dressing room when he heard a knock at the front door. It was a sheepish knock, so soft it could barely be heard unless one had extremely keen senses. Fortunately, Jean-Claude's hearing was supernaturally keen, as were his instincts. He looked up sharply, suspecting trouble. His dinner guests were not yet due, and he had heard no horse and carriage on the drive. Whoever was knocking must have walked.

Jean-Claude listened intently as his butler opened the front door and spoke to the interloper. He frowned and swiftly finished adjusting his cravat. He recognized the second voice as that of the chief constable, a man of humble origins and mean intellect. He was stubborn as a bulldog with a bone, for all that, and therefore not to be underestimated.

The butler appeared in the door of his dressing room. "Chief Constable Jean Boucher to see you, sir," Henri Deschamp intoned with a meaningful nod.

"*Tres bien*, Deschamp. Please escort him to the study. I will be down directly," Jean-Claude said.

Moving slowly to give himself time to think, Jean-Claude shrugged himself into his jacket and walked composedly down the grand staircase. Deschamp opened the study door and Jean-

Claude stepped inside. Chief Constable Boucher stumbled awkwardly to his feet, pulling off his cap.

"Chief Constable, *bonjour*. How may I be of service?" Jean-Claude asked smoothly, moving with the grace of a striking wolf to the sofas grouped around the fireplace. He waved the police officer to a seat.

"I . . . I'm sorry to intrude, Monsieur Dubois, especially on the night of your dinner party, but it is my duty to investigate every detail of a crime," the chief constable said wretchedly, seating himself on the edge of the couch.

"Pardon, *monsieur*? I do not understand," Jean-Claude said, stepping to the drinks cabinet. "Would you care for a drink?"

"Can't drink when I'm on duty," Boucher muttered.

"*Non*? Very well." Jean-Claude sank gracefully into an armchair. "Perhaps you could explain what brings you here? Succinctly, if you please, Chief Constable. I have guests arriving for dinner in twenty minutes."

"It's about them two deaths out on the prairie," Boucher said. "Father and son were both found with their throats torn out, three weeks apart. Folks say wolves done them in, but Madame Gagnier, the wife and mother, she is sure it was murder. She claims Monsieur Fontaine, a lumber baron who offered the family money for their land, hired an assassin to kill her husband when he refused to sell the property. After the father died, the lumber baron approached the son, and the son also refused to sell. Now both of them are dead, and the widow thinks she's going to be next. She's got some bee in her bonnet about the assassin being a loup-garou—that is to say, a werewolf."

"I *have* heard of the loup-garou, constable. I do not require a definition," Jean-Claude murmured politely. "Do go on with your story."

"It's all nonsense to my mind. Everyone knows werewolves are just a fairy tale," Boucher said hastily. "But Madame Gagnier insists I treat the killings like a murder investigation. She's been in my office every day for the last week to see what progress I've made. What with the deaths taking place so soon after father and son refused to sell their land, I thought it my duty to check up on them."

"It is laudable, Monsieur Boucher, that you take your duties seriously," Jean-Claude replied. "But I am still puzzled by your presence here. What does this tale have to do with me? You have ten minutes left."

The chief constable gulped and said in a rush, "Someone told Madame Gagnier that the members of the Dubois clan are loups-garous. She has accused you, the head of the Dubois clan, of the murder of her husband and son."

Jean-Claude threw back his dark head and laughed heartily. When he caught his breath, he said, "A loup-garou? Me? Why yes, constable, I am a loup-garou and so is my butler. And my cook is a zombie and my cousin Claudette is a vampire. *Really*, constable, you came all this way for a fairy story?"

Chief Constable Boucher turned bright red and stared at the floor. Then he stared at the ceiling. Finally, he looked Jean-Claude in the eye and said, "I have to do my duty, sir. Where were you on the night of May fifteenth and again on the night of June sixth?"

"I will have to check my calendar to be sure of my whereabouts on May fifteenth. On June sixth I was here at home, entertaining the Duchess of Southbury, a distant cousin who was visiting from England," Jean-Claude said. "She brought a large house party with her, at least fifteen or twenty people. Any of them can vouch for my whereabouts. As for May fifteenth . . ." He rose and went to his desk, inlaid with intricate patterns in dark- and light-colored wood. He opened the top drawer and took out his calendar. "Let me see . . . Ah, yes. On May fifteenth, I was in Montreal, spending the weekend with my Aunt Jessica and Uncle Claude." He showed the police officer the notation in his calendar. "They will be more than happy to vouch for me."

Outside, the thud of hooves and the rattle of approaching carriages heralded the arrival of Jean-Claude's dinner guests. It was half past the hour—time for this entertaining interlude to end. Jean-Claude rose, and the chief constable rose with him.

"I hope this talk has settled your mind, monsieur," Jean-Claude said politely.

"I apologize for intruding, monsieur," Boucher said, avoiding the question. Jean-Claude knew the chief constable still suspected him of murder. After all, the man was stubborn.

As Jean-Claude escorted him toward the servant's entrance at the back, Boucher said musingly, "It's a funny thing, those deaths. Father and son both get their throats torn out by wolves, exactly three weeks apart."

"You must look for your mythical assassin among the wolf packs, constable," said Jean-Claude, opening a side door for his unwelcome visitor.

Boucher turned in the doorway and met his gaze squarely. "I intend to do that, Monsieur Dubois."

"Good man," Jean-Claude said. "And now, farewell."

ASSASSIN

Boucher excused himself and walked humbly—perhaps a bit too humbly?—through the twilit kitchen garden toward the road. Jean-Claude watched until he was out of sight.

The butler, Deschamp, materialized soundlessly beside his cousin and employer. "Is Boucher going to be a problem?" he murmured.

Jean-Claude shook his head. "Not at all. Show my guests into the drawing room and serve them drinks, please. Tell them I have been delayed by some unfinished business."

"Very good, sir," Deschamp said impassively. As he turned away, he added: "*Bon appétit.*"

Jean-Claude stepped out into the twilight and quietly closed the door behind him. He smiled, and his incisors lengthened.

"A loup-garou assassin," he murmured as he loped after the retreating chief constable. "What an imagination that poor man has!"

The words became a growl as Jean-Claude dropped to all fours and changed shape without missing a stride. He really loved his work.

24

The Seventh Window

Veronica hated her confined life. Her domineering father would not let her go to dances or introduce her into society. After the death of her mother, the dark-haired beauty became a virtual prisoner in her own home, attending to her father's every whim and listening silently to his nightly tantrums. Veronica's life was unbearable, and she desperately sought escape from the lovely mansion that was her prison.

Escape came in the autumn of 1890, when the mysterious Mr. Rutherford began calling on Veronica after her father had retired to his rooms for the evening. Heretofore, she had only heard rumors about the rich, elderly miser. The people in town said he lived alone in a decrepit old mansion on the far side of town with only one deaf servant to cook his meals and tend to his meager needs. Mr. Rutherford never came to town for any reason. His deaf servant did all his banking and shopping for him.

Once a month a mysterious shipment of unlabeled boxes arrived at the train station for the rich miser. The delivery man was instructed to take the shipment to the mansion and leave the large, heavy boxes on the stoop. The mansion door never opened while the delivery man was on the grounds. Folks in town frequently debated what those boxes might contain, but no one was invited into the mansion to find out.

THE SEVENTH WINDOW

On his first visit, Mr. Rutherford stayed for a half hour and made small talk with Veronica in the approved society fashion. He was a tall, white-haired gentleman with a cultured voice and hard black eyes. His dark suit had a faintly chemical smell about it that Veronica found repellent. But he was the only suitor who dared brave her father's wrath, so what choice did she have?

Once a week for the next two months, Mr. Rutherford paid court to the lovely eighteen-year-old. The blue-eyed, dark-haired beauty used every wile at her disposal to attract the old man, so desperate was she for escape. *Please, God, let him propose,* she prayed each night. And propose he did, to her intense relief.

Veronica's father was furious when he learned of her clandestine courtship. He threw her bags onto the lawn and locked the door behind her when her betrothed arrived to take her to their town hall wedding. Disowned forever, Veronica resolved to forget her old life as her bridegroom drove away from her former home.

Veronica's new resolve was shaken when she caught her first glimpse of decrepit old Rutherford mansion on the far side of town. It was surrounded by a ruined hulk of a garden and bizarrely segmented cracked brick walkways. Detritus was piled so high against the double front doors that the newlyweds were forced to enter the mansion through the portal at the back.

Rutherford disappeared into the depths of the mansion without a word, leaving Veronica in the ruined back hallway with the elderly deaf maidservant. Veronica almost choked on the horrible chemical smell that pervaded the whole house. The stale dusty air made her sneeze, and her lovely blue eyes watered unattractively as she followed the maidservant through the worn-out hallway. They climbed a magnificent, cobweb-encrusted staircase and entered a large bedroom on the second floor.

The servant dropped Veronica's bag beside the fireplace and withdrew, leaving the bereft bride staring at the tattered tapestries, the worn-out chair coverings, and the faded quilt on the large canopy bed that rose like a bier in the center of the room.

When Veronica pulled aside the tattered bed curtains, she was suddenly enveloped by tiny white moths that fluttered sickeningly around her. She gasped and flailed at the creatures, their tiny wings brushing her face and neck like grasping fingers. The moths vanished as suddenly as they had appeared, and Veronica pressed a hand to her pounding heart, the chemical smell strong in her nostrils.

All at once, Veronica's eyes focused on the large faded bed she shortly would be sharing with her new husband. The idea made her stomach roil, and she lunged for the shutters that covered the window, longing for fresh air. But the window catch was rusted shut, and she could not open it.

Defeated, Veronica turned back into the room. Her eye was caught suddenly by a large portrait hanging above the fireplace. A lovely blonde bride leaned her elbow against a marble pillar, her lovely cheek resting on her hand. Her bridal veil cascaded around her intricately arranged hair, and a marvelous necklace of rubies enwreathed her smooth neck. Her free hand lay on the head of a large French poodle. Tiny white slippers peeped out from underneath her magnificent white dress. Veronica stared entranced at the portrait and then glanced ruefully down at her own wedding suit of conservative blue and gray.

At that moment, a pair of folding doors on the far side of the room slid open. Veronica realized with a start that her bedroom must adjoin that of Rutherford, for he stood observing her from the doorway. "If you would be so good as to join me?" he said politely. "Supper is served."

Veronica swallowed and nodded. She passed through the folding doors and looked apprehensively around her husband's apartment. Rutherford's room was larger than hers. It was quickly apparent that he spent much of his time there, for the room was a combination study and bedroom. Books lined two walls, and against the third wall stood a small dining table and a hideous iron stove. The bed with its dusty spread and sagging springs was relegated to a far corner, as if it was of small importance.

The newlyweds sat in silence while the deaf maidservant served a mouthwatering meal. Veronica broke the silence to inquire about the fancy portrait above her fireplace.

"She was my first wife," Rutherford said abruptly, in a tone that brooked no further questions. Veronica gulped and thereafter stayed silent. When the meal was done, Rutherford stood politely and motioned for Veronica to go to her room.

Veronica departed with racing heart, aware that it was her wedding night and that she had married a man she did not love. The faintly sweet chemical smell assaulted her nostrils afresh as she entered her apartment. The folding doors closed behind her and bile rose suddenly in her throat. Stomach churning, she was overwhelmed by a desire for fresh air. Veronica bolted for the hallway and ran down the stairs and through the decrepit hall to the back door.

Veronica's hand was on the knob when the elderly maidservant appeared from nowhere and caught hold of her arm in a gentle but ruthless grip. Veronica stared at the blank-faced woman in sudden fear, and then she became aware of a clap of thunder overhead and the pounding of rain against the roof of the mansion. Wind shook the house from top to bottom as the maidservant withdrew, leaving Veronica alone in the storm-beleaguered hallway.

Resigned to her fate, Veronica went upstairs and put on her nightgown. She sat by the fire to wait for the appearance of her new husband, breathing deeply of the dusty, stifling air inside the worn-out room. Slowly her dark lashes sank against her cheeks, and she fell into a deep sleep.

In the early hours of the morning, Rutherford came silently through the folding doors carrying a small flashlight and a tape measure. He regarded his sleeping bride thoughtfully as she lay in the chair by the flickering fire. Then he looked up at the portrait above the fireplace. He seemed to be making some kind of mental comparison between his former bride and the new one. Then he took the tape and began measuring his sleeping bride from head to hips, from hip to knee, from knee to toe. Length of arm. Length of feet. Length of fingers. Length of neck. He fingered a dark tress of hair as if assessing its texture. So light was his touch that Veronica never awoke. Measurements completed, Rutherford withdrew as silently as he had arrived.

Veronica woke the next morning when the servant arrived with breakfast. She begged the maid to open the window shutters

174

to let in the fresh air. The deaf woman went next door to consult with her master and then silently returned to open the shutters. A moment later, Rutherford opened the folding doors. Veronica's heart thudded in belated panic. She had slept through her wedding night, and now her hour of wifely reckoning was upon her. But Rutherford merely inquired after her sleep and asked her to join him for lunch. Veronica's panic changed to puzzlement. It seemed her elderly husband did not wish a physical relationship with his new wife.

And so it proved in the days that followed. Veronica took meals with her elderly husband, who then withdrew to his own pursuits, leaving her alone to read or sew. She spent a good bit of her first week wandering through the decrepit mansion. On the morning after her wedding, Veronica explored the dusty, unfurnished rooms with shuttered windows on the first floor. She found a stack of paintings in a corner covered by a dusty sheet, but none were as fine as the bridal portrait in her bedroom. The next day she explored the unoccupied bedrooms on the second floor, but there was little to interest her, and she soon grew bored and withdrew to her apartment to read.

On her third day, Veronica investigated the third floor. As she turned the corner of the third-floor landing, she stepped into a sunbeam filled with hundreds and hundreds of white moths. They fluttered around her, suffocating her just as they had the first night she arrived. Veronica shrieked and batted at them, finally covering her head with her arms and fleeing upward to get away.

As Veronica reached the top step, dry wings brushed her dark hair. Looking up, she saw a stuffed seagull hanging from a wire at the top of the stair. When she looked down the hallway, hundreds of glass eyes stared at her from every nook and cranny along its length. A stuffed fox sniffed the air. A red-jacketed monkey sat on a chair. An owl perched on a log. A cat lounged on a cushion.

Everywhere Veronica looked, dead animals glared back at her. It appeared her new husband had a mania for taxidermy. Well, at least this explained the mysterious shipments that came each month on the train. Rutherford was obviously collecting dead animals to stuff. It was a revolting obsession, but there was nothing mysterious about it. At least it explained the moths.

As the weeks passed, Veronica realized that she had replaced one form of captivity with another. True, her new husband did not scream at her. But she had no more freedom of thought and movement now than she had with her autocratic father. Less, even, for she was rarely allowed to walk in the weed-choked garden. She spent her days reading books, wandering alone through the rooms of the mansion, and eating rich meals because her husband thought she needed fattening up.

The maidservant spoke not a word to her new mistress, tending silently to her needs and appearing unexpectedly whenever Veronica wandered too close to her husband's taxidermy workshop. Although Rutherford never forbade her from going up to the third floor, Veronica sensed that her husband and his maidservant did not want her roaming there.

As lonely month followed lonely month, Veronica realized she must escape her constricted life or go insane. She wanted to be free of the elderly miser who ignored her, free of this horror house with its dead animals and moths and dust, free of the maid who was more a keeper than a servant. But Veronica had no way of affecting her escape. The servant did all the shopping, so Veronica had no money. She was never allowed to visit the town. And where could she go if she ran away? Her father would not take her back, and she had no other family.

One evening, as Veronica sat sewing by the fire, futilely running escape options through her anxious mind, her eye fell on the bride's portrait above the fireplace. She stared at the rubies adorning the throat of Rutherford's first wife and realized that those rubies must be someplace in this house. The miserly Rutherford would not have disposed of something so valuable. If she found those rubies, Veronica could go far away and make a new life for herself.

From that moment, Veronica began searching the mansion room by room for the rubies. She would send the maidservant on long errands and then tap on the walls, look under furniture, and search in and around the stuffed animals that filled the third-floor rooms. Veronica hated those animals, so full of dust and chemical smells. They felt so dead when she touched them, preserved for all eternity in a ghastly resurrection that felt beyond redemption. But she touched them anyway, for it occurred to her that a stuffed animal might make a good hiding place for the rubies.

One evening, when the maidservant was sent on an errand for her master, Veronica slipped into Rutherford's taxidermy workshop to search for the rubies and saw that Rutherford was working on a new project. The upper portion of a wax head sat on the workbench, its forehead and dark-lashed eyes already in place. The dark blue glass eyes struck a deep, negative chord in Veronica. A shiver ran down her spine as she gazed into the glass eyes, trying to recall where she'd seen them.

177

The clock struck in the hallway, and she realized she was wasting precious time. The maidservant would return shortly. This might be Veronica's only chance to search the workshop. She turned her back on the model and hurriedly searched the room, racing away at the last minute when she heard the back door slam as the maidservant returned to the mansion.

Later that evening, Veronica was taking a rare stroll through the ruined garden when she was struck by an oddity in the construction of the mansion's third floor. In her explorations, she had discovered three big rooms on each side of the third-floor hallway. Each room had two shuttered windows. Three times two made six windows, which were cut into the north and south sides of the mansion. So why were there *seven* shuttered windows on the south side? Veronica counted the third-floor windows several times, and each time she came up with an extra window. Veronica's heart pounded with excitement as she realized that the seventh window must be inside a secret room behind her husband's workshop. And therein, she was suddenly sure, she would find the rubies.

Over the next few weeks, Veronica slipped to the third floor whenever she could to search for the hidden room. She tapped the walls and pressed the molding and inspected every inch of the hallway and workshop. She was about to give up in despair when her questing fingers found a flexible place in the molding at the far end of the third-floor hallway. When she pressed it, a panel slid aside, revealing a large metal door with a combination lock. Hearing footsteps on the staircase, she hastily pressed the molding again and the door slid shut. She hurried to the sniffing fox and stood inspecting it as the suspicious maidservant entered the hall and beckoned to Veronica.

That night, Rutherford called for wine to be served with dinner. They never drank wine, and Veronica eyed its appearance with suspicion.

"Do you know what today is?" her husband asked in an unusually jovial tone. Veronica shook her head. "My dear, it is our anniversary," Rutherford said. "We should drink to our happy union." His eyes were bright with anticipation as he poured red wine into her glass and then fixed himself a tonic and gin. "To us," he said, raising his glass.

Then Rutherford's left arm jerked and the glass fell out of his hand, shattering on the floor as he clutched at his arm. A moment later, he toppled over, dead of a heart attack. Veronica leapt to his side, but it was too late. She stared at his lifeless open eyes, so much like those of his stuffed creatures. Then Veronica called for the maidservant and sent her to summon the doctor. In the hubbub that followed, the nuptial glass of wine stood forgotten until the maidservant found it the next morning and poured it out.

It wasn't until her husband's body was carried away that Veronica realized she no longer needed the rubies. She was a rich widow, and the whole estate was hers to do with as she pleased.

After the funeral, Veronica pensioned off the maidservant handsomely for her years of service and sent her away. Then she put the house up for sale and prepared to move to Richmond to start a new life far away from the old.

While cleaning out her husband's rooms, Veronica found a lock combination hidden inside an old-fashioned pocket watch: "Twenty-four left, five right, sixteen left, nine right." It was then that Veronica remembered the secret door and the missing rubies. She had been so busy with the paperwork and her husband's funeral that she'd forgotten them completely.

Overwhelmed by a sudden desire to find those amazing rubies and take them to Richmond as a reward for her year of misery, Veronica went to the third floor and entered the combination into the lock on the secret door. When she opened the door, Veronica was overwhelmed by the chemical smell in the room. It was even stronger than the smell from her dead husband's workshop. No light came through the shuttered seventh window, so Veronica fetched a lantern from her husband's workshop.

As she re-entered the secret room, Veronica gasped in astonishment. The lantern illuminated a life-size replica of the bride's portrait from her room. It was a magnificent painting, more finely detailed than the smaller portrait. Gradually, Veronica's wonder turned to unease. Something wasn't right about the picture. A shudder crept across her skin and cold beads of sweat formed on her arms and neck when she realized that the scene in front of her was three-dimensional. A shadow flickered underneath the white French poodle, and the light glittered off the rubies at the bride's throat. Veronica swallowed dryly and reached out her hand. Her fingers touched glass.

Horror overwhelmed the new widow as she realized what she beheld. Mr. Rutherford's mania for taxonomy had driven him over the edge of sanity. Here, preserved in chemicals and glass, was the murdered body of his first wife.

A memory flashed before Veronica's inner eye. Once more she saw the partially completed wax head with the dark-lashed blue eyes, and she realized those blue eyes were hers. "No!" Veronica screamed, lashing out blindly with the lantern as she envisioned her own body preserved inside the life-size glass box. The sharp edge of her lantern struck the case and the glass shattered inward, coating the bride and the poodle inside the box. As fresh air hit the corpse, the wedding gown crumbled to dust, leaving a bare skeleton seated beside the marble column. The sparkling red rubies around her throat were the same shade as the poisoned wine Rutherford had poured into Veronica's glass on the night of their anniversary.

25

Estrid

"Estrid. Her name is Estrid!"

Gregory shouted the words aloud to the sleeping city. He hugged himself in glee and waltzed along the cobblestone road until he reached his small room at the back of the exclusive inn where he worked as a journeyman chef.

Gregory had just achieved journeyman status, and it came with an increase in salary. He was delighted, for now he could take a wife and begin his family. And Estrid was the lucky woman who would make him the happiest of men. The young chef chortled merrily and kicked his heels in a spasm of sheer delight. Maybe he was a bit of a fool to have fallen in love with a girl he'd never met, but Gregory didn't care. Time would take care of that problem.

Gregory had been making blood sausage for a gathering at the inn when he'd seen Estrid for the first time. He was mixing pig blood into the bowl with the other ingredients when a red flash outside the window caught his eye. Gregory looked outside and saw a woman walking down the lantern-lit cobblestone street. Her knee-length red hair swirled around her like a cloak. The woman's form was dainty and well-rounded in all the right places. Gregory could not see her face, but anyone with such gorgeous red hair must be beautiful. He couldn't take his eyes off the woman's hair.

Gregory watched until the woman disappeared around a corner. Only then did he realize he'd spilled most of the pig blood on the floor.

From that moment, Gregory longed to meet the red-haired woman, but night followed long night without a glimpse of her—until tonight. Gregory had been making blood pudding for tomorrow's special luncheon when he glimpsed the red-haired woman walking down the street in the light of the gas lamps. He put the pudding in the cold room, hands shaking with nerves, and bolted outside. To his relief, the woman was just turning the corner ahead of him. Gregory followed, calling, "Lady, please wait!" But she didn't hear him. She stayed a block ahead of him, moving swiftly through the twists and turns of the old city. Gregory's heart was thundering from so much unexpected exercise, and he was clutching a stitch in his side by the time the red-haired woman stopped suddenly before a door, turned a key in the lock, and slipped inside. He hobbled up the steps and knocked. After a moment, a lovely female voice called to him through the door, "Who is it?"

"It is I, Gregory, the journeyman chef from the inn," he called through the door. "Lovely lady, I have seen you passing the inn and I wish to court you. I make a fine salary and would be a very good husband. Lady, may I meet you?"

To his delight, the woman replied, "I have seen you at the inn, Gregory the chef, and I would like to meet you. But I cannot come out this evening. My parents are ill. Could you return tomorrow?"

Gregory shivered in delight. "I could come tomorrow. But lovely lady, at least tell me your name!"

Through the door, the woman cooed, "Estrid. My name is Estrid."

That night, Gregory dreamed of his new love. He saw Estrid walking away from him down the road that led to the woods outside town. Her blood-red hair floated around her like a cloak, gleaming in the starlight. He followed her, longing to see her lovely face, but she was always just a few yards ahead of him, following a winding path toward a dark cottage surrounded by tall pines. And then the morning sunlight woke him, and it was time to go to work.

Gregory hummed to himself as he worked. The usually temperamental journeyman actually joked with the kitchen boys, and he didn't even scold the server when he dropped a plate of salmon on the floor. The staff was amazed by the chef's good humor. But Gregory's mind wasn't on his work. He kept seeing Estrid's blood-red hair swaying around her as she walked home in the lamplight. He would see her tonight! How would he make it through the day?

The hours crawled slowly by, but at last Gregory was standing in his best suit, clutching a bouquet of blood-red roses. He raised his hand to knock, but before his knuckles brushed the wood, Estrid's voice spoke from behind the door.

"Gregory, I am sorry," she said. "My parents are still ill and I cannot go out with you tonight."

Gregory blinked in surprise. How had Estrid known he was here? But his surprise was swallowed swiftly by disappointment.

"I am sorry to hear they are ill," he said politely. "I have flowers for you. Will you open the door so I can give them to you in person?"

But Estrid said, "I hear my mother calling to me. I had better go to her. Would you leave the flowers by the door? And would you come tomorrow night instead, so we can meet?"

Her voice was so sweet and delicate that Gregory was smitten anew. He could wait one more night to meet his love. "Of course, my lady. I will see you tomorrow night."

"Good dreams, my Gregory," Estrid cooed through the door.

Gregory left the blood-red roses on the doorstep and floated home. "Estrid," he whispered to the wind. "Her name is Estrid." He tumbled into bed and dreamed at once of the lovely red-haired woman, always walking away from him down the cobblestone streets. All night long, he followed her through the twists and turns of the city and then out into the woods, down the dark path to the cottage in the pines. In his dream, he peered through a crack and saw Estrid with her back to him, stirring a pot of blood-red soup before the fire. It was the same color as her long, lovely red hair. *Turn around, Estrid,* Gregory willed. *Let me see your face.* But a sunbeam slanted through his window and woke him before Estrid finished stirring her soup.

Around noon, Gregory tossed the last of the tomato slices into the pot and put it over the fire to slowly simmer into a deep, thick tomato soup to be served with the supper that night. The blood-red soup looked so much like the soup he'd seen in his dream of Estrid that Gregory decided it must be a sign. She was making soup; he was making soup. They were meant for each other! He sighed romantically and forgot to scold the kitchen boy for forgetting to fill the wood box.

Donning his best suit once again after the kitchen closed for the night, Gregory made his way through the twisted streets to

Estrid's door. He knocked boldly, and Estrid answered at once, speaking through the door. "Gregory, my father is very poorly. You cannot come in."

Gregory's heart sank into his shoes. Estrid was avoiding him. She did not want to meet her clumsy suitor. As if she could read his mind, Estrid cooed, "Of course I must meet you, Gregory. I just cannot meet you now. But at midnight I will come to the fountain in the square beside the inn. Meet me there tonight, as I have met you in your dreams these last two evenings."

Gregory's eyes widened. "You sent me those dreams?"

"Of course," cooed the lovely voice. "You are my true love. I could not be with you in the flesh, so I came to you in your dreams."

A shiver ran down Gregory's spine. He was astonished at this sign of power from the delicate woman with the blood-red hair. And such a woman wanted him, a journeyman chef? It seemed like a miracle. "I will meet you by the fountain," he promised the lovely voice behind the door. And he danced all the way back to the inn, to the amused delight of all who passed him in the street.

Gregory spent the next two hours pacing back and forth in the square, waiting for Estrid to appear. Eventually, he tired of all the walking and sank down on a bench to wait. His eyes grew heavy as midnight approached. Gregory toppled slowly onto the seat of the bench and fell into a lovely dream. He was walking down the winding path through the woods toward the cottage. Firelight spilled through the partially opened door, and he could see Estrid bent over the steaming pot of blood-red soup, her red hair gleaming. As if she sensed his approach,

ESTRID

Estrid called over her shoulder, "Come in, Gregory. I have been expecting you!"

All around the square, the world went silent and too still. Even the wind ceased batting the dead autumn leaves hither and thither across the cobbles. The gas lamps shivered behind their glass as a figure with flowing blood-red hair floated soundlessly down from the sky above the square and landed beside the sleeping Gregory. "Hello, love," Estrid cooed as her hair spilled across his prone form and writhed and wrapped itself around him. Each lock of hair sprouted slitted golden snake eyes and sank sharp fangs into the dreaming chef's neck to suck and suck his thick red blood.

In Gregory's dream, Estrid turned away from the fire at last to face her suitor. To his horror, the transfixed journeyman beheld the twisted, fanged visage of a hag. "I am happy to meet you," Estrid cooed.

Gregory screamed and tried to wake himself. But there was nothing to go back to. Every drop of blood had been drained from his sleeping body. In his last frantic moment of life, Gregory felt the dream Estrid wrap cloying arms around his soul. Then the hag opened her fanged mouth and bit down.

Resources

Asfar, Dan, and Edrick Thay. *Ghost Stories of America*. Edmonton, AB: Ghost House Books, 2001.

Bain, Gordon A. *The Edge of the Firelight*. Seattle: CreateSpace Independent Publishing Platform, 2012.

Battle, Kemp P. *Great American Folklore*. New York: Doubleday & Company, Inc., 1986.

Botkin, B. A., ed. *A Treasury of American Folklore*. New York: Crown, 1944.

Boyle, Virginia Frazer, and A. B. Frost. *Devil Tales: Black Americana Folk-Lore*. New York: Harper & Brothers Publishers, 1900.

Brown, Alan. *Stories from the Haunted South*. Jackson: University Press of Mississippi, 2004.

Brunvand, Jan Harold. *Be Afraid, Be Very Afraid*. New York: W. W. Norton & Company, 2004.

———. *The Choking Doberman and Other Urban Legends*. New York: W. W. Norton & Company, 1984.

———. *Curses! Broiled Again*. New York: W. W. Norton & Company, 1989.

———. *The Vanishing Hitchhiker*. New York: W. W. Norton & Company, 1981.

Caperton, Helena Lefroy. *Legends of Virginia*. Richmond: Garrett & Massie, Inc., 1950.

Christensen, Jo-Anne. *Campfire Ghost Stories*. Edmonton, AB: Ghost House Books, 2002.

———. *More Ghost Stories of Saskatchewan*. Edmonton, AB: Lone Pine Publishing, 2000.

Coffin, Tristram P., and Hennig Cohen, eds. *Folklore in America*. New York: Doubleday & AMP, 1966.

———. *Folklore from the Working Folk of America*. New York: Doubleday, 1973.

Cohen, Daniel, and Susan Cohen. *Hauntings & Horrors*. New York: Dutton Children's Books, 2002.

Craughwell, Thomas J. *Urban Legends: 666 Absolutely True Stories That Happened to a Friend . . . Of a Friend . . . Of a Friend*. New York: Black Dog and Leventhal Publishers, Inc., 2002.

Dorson, Richard M. *America in Legend*. New York: Pantheon Books, 1973.

Downer, Deborah L., ed. *Classic American Ghost Stories*. Little Rock, AR: August House Publishers, Inc., 2005.

Editors of *Life*. *The Life Treasury of American Folklore*. New York: Time Inc., 1961.

Eldredge, Kimberly. *Scary & Silly Campfire Stories: Fifteen Spooky & Silly Tales*. Vols. 1 and 2. Chino Valley, AZ: Outdoor Princess Productions, LLC, 2012.

Resources

Erdoes, Richard, and Alfonso Ortiz, eds. *American Indian Myths and Legends*. New York: Pantheon Books, 1984.

Flanagan, J. T., and A. P. Hudson. *The American Folk Reader*. New York: A. S. Barnes & Co., 1958.

Forgey, William, M.D. *Campfire Stories: Things That Go Bump in the Night*. Guilford, CT: Globe Pequot Press, 1985.

Gibbons, Faye. *Hook Moon Night*. New York: Morrow Junior Books, 1997.

Hanson, Bob, and Bill Roemmich. *Stories for the Campfire*. Martinsville, IN: American Camping Association, 1983.

Harold, Jim. *Jim Harold's Campfire: True Ghost Stories*. Pompton Plains, NJ: New Page Books, 2011.

Harriot, Ray. *Stories for Around the Campfire*. Laurel, MD: Campfire Publishing Company, 1986.

———. *More Stories for Around the Campfire*. Laurel, MD: Campfire Publishing Company, 1998.

Hauck, Dennis William. *Haunted Places: The National Directory*. New York: Penguin Books, 1994.

Holub, Joan. *The Haunted States of America*. New York: Aladdin Paperbacks, 2001.

Jones, Louis C. *Things That Go Bump in the Night*. Syracuse, NY: Syracuse University Press Edition, 1983.

Laine, Tanner. *Campfire Stories*. Lubbock, TX: Ranch House Publications, 1965.

Leach, Marcia. *The Rainbow Book of American Folk Tales and Legends*. New York: The World Publishing Co., 1958.

Leeming, David, and Jake Page. *Myths, Legends, and Folktales of America: An Anthology*. New York: Oxford University Press, 1999.

Mott, A. S. *Ghost Stories of America*. Vol. II. Edmonton, AB: Ghost House Books, 2003.

Norman, Michael, and Beth Scott. *Historic Haunted America*. New York: Tor Books, 1995.

Olson, Arielle North, and Howard Schwartz. *Ask the Bones: Scary Stories from Around the World*. New York: Puffin Books, 2002.

———. *More Bones: Scary Stories from Around the World*. New York: Puffin Books, 2008.

Peck, Catherine, ed. *A Treasury of North American Folk Tales*. New York: W. W. Norton, 1998.

Penn-Coughin, O. *They're Coming for You: Scary Stories That Scream to Be Read*. Bend, OR: You Come Too Publishing, 2008.

———. *They're Coming for You 2: More Scary Stories That Scream to Be Read*. Bend, OR: You Come Too Publishing, 2010.

Polley, J., ed. *American Folklore and Legend*. New York: Reader's Digest Association, 1978.

Reevy, Tony. *Ghost Train!* Lynchburg, VA: TLC Publishing, 1998.

Roberts, Nancy. *Ghosts from the Coast*. Chapel Hill: University of North Carolina Press, 2001.

———. *The Haunted South*. Columbia: University of South Carolina Press, 1988.

Rule, Leslie. *Coast to Coast Ghosts*. Kansas City, MO: Andrews McMeel Publishing, 2001.

San Souci, Robert D. *Short & Shivery: Thirty Chilling Tales*. New York: Yearling, 1987.

Schwartz, Alvin. *Scary Stories to Tell in the Dark*. New York: HarperCollins, 1981.

———. *More Scary Stories to Tell in the Dark*. New York: HarperCollins, 1984.

———. *Scary Stories 3: More Tales to Chill Your Bones*. New York: HarperCollins, 1991.

Skinner, Charles M. *American Myths and Legends*. Vol. 1. Philadelphia: J. B. Lippincott, 1903.

———. *Myths and Legends of Our Own Land*. Vols. 1 and 2. Philadelphia: J. B. Lippincott, 1896.

Smith, Barbara. *Ghost Stories of the Rocky Mountains*. Vol. I. Edmonton, AB: Lone Pine Publishing, 1999.

———. *Ghost Stories of the Rocky Mountains*. Vol. II. Edmonton, AB: Lone Pine Publishing, 2003.

Spence, Lewis. *North American Indians: Myths and Legends Series*. London: Bracken Books, 1985.

Students of Haskell Institute. *Myths, Legends, Superstitions of North American Indian Tribes*. Cherokee, NC: Cherokee Publications, 1995.

Thay, Edrick. *Ghost Stories of the Old South*. Edmonton, AB: Ghost House Books, 2003.

Welch, R. C. *Scary Stories for Sleep-Overs*. New York: RGA Publishing Group, Inc., 1991.

Young, Richard, and Judy Dockrey Young. *Favorite Scary Stories of American Children*. Little Rock, AR: August House Publishers, 1990.

———. *Ghost Stories from the American Southwest*. Little Rock, AR: August House Publishers, 1991.

Zeitlin, Steven J., Amy J. Kotkin, and Holly Cutting Baker. *A Celebration of American Family Folklore*. New York: Pantheon Books, 1982.

About the Author

Author S. E. Schlosser has been telling stories since she was a child, when games of "let's pretend" quickly built themselves into full-length stories. A graduate of the Institute of Children's Literature and Rutgers University, she also created and maintains www.AmericanFolklore.net, where she shares a wealth of stories from all fifty states, some dating from the origins of America.

About the Illustrator

Artist Paul Hoffman trained in painting and printmaking. His first extensive illustration work on assignment was in Egypt, drawing ancient wall reliefs for the University of Chicago. His work graces books of many genres—including, children's titles, textbooks, short story collections, natural history volumes, and numerous cookbooks. For *More Spooky Campfire Tales*, he employed a scratchboard technique and an active imagination.